THE FIGHT INSIDE

THE FIGHT INSIDE

Winning the Battle Between Your Ego and True Spirit

LYNETTE EDDY, MSW

The Fight Inside

Winning the Battle Between Your Ego and True Spirit

Lynette Eddy

Published by Lynette Eddy, MSW

ISBN: 979-8-9874191-0-6

Open-Heart Mindfulness Approach® is a registered trademark owned by Lynette Eddy.

Copyright © 2022 by Lynette Eddy, MSW. All rights reserved. No part of this publication may be reproduced, distributed, or transmitted in any form or by any means, including photocopying, recording, or other electronic or mechanical methods, without the prior written permission of the publisher, except in the case of brief quotations embodied in critical reviews and certain other noncommercial uses permitted by copyright law. For further information, please contact the author at eddylynette@gmail.com.

BONUS

OPEN-HEART MINDFULNESS TOOLBOX

This book's concepts can help you avoid a lot of unnecessary suffering and live a more intentional life. To help incorporate these ideas into your daily life, I have created the Open-Heart Mindfulness Toolbox. Here you will find tips, tools, and suggestions for bringing a greater sense of well-being and balance to your life. Download your **FREE** copy of the Toolbox here:

www.LynetteEddy.com/toolbox

CONTENTS

Introduction	ix
PART ONE WHEN LIFE HITS YOU HARD	**1**
CHAPTER ONE: My Ordinary Instant	3
CHAPTER TWO: Motherless Child	17
CHAPTER THREE: Life in Truckee	39
CHAPTER FOUR: Processing	49
CHAPTER FIVE: The Voice of the Ego	59
PART TWO TURNING A NEGATIVE INTO A POSITIVE	**69**
CHAPTER SIX: Future Social Worker	71
CHAPTER SEVEN: Brian's Story	81
CHAPTER EIGHT: The Path Forward	91
CHAPTER NINE: New Directions	113
CHAPTER TEN: Everyone Needs a Home	121

PART THREE   SOUL TO SOUL — 135

CHAPTER ELEVEN: Tanzania — 137

CHAPTER TWELVE: Walking Trees — 149

CHAPTER THIRTEEN: Lost at Sea – Lost on Land – Greece — 155

CHAPTER FOURTEEN: Ghana — 163

CHAPTER FIFTEEN: Blue Zones — 169

CHAPTER SIXTEEN: Shedding the Earth Suit — 175

Acknowledgments — 182
About the Author — 183

INTRODUCTION

A grandmother is teaching her granddaughter about life. "A fight is going on inside me," she said to the girl. "It is a terrible fight and it is between two wolves. One is evil-he is filled with anger, envy, sorrow, regret, greed, arrogance, lies and superiority." She continued, "The other is good-he is filled with joy, peace, love, hope, kindness, truth, and compassion. The same fight is going on in all of us."

The granddaughter thought for a minute and then asked, "Which one will win?" The grandmother simply replied, "The one you feed."

BASED ON AN AMERICAN NATIVE FOLKTALE

* * *

In the spring of 2010, my husband, Bob, died by suicide. As you can imagine, this devastated our family and, in the aftermath, we were left with more questions than answers.

A year after his death and while I was completing my master's degree in social work, I tried to clinically label the mental state Bob was in before he took his life. While not able to diagnose him from the DSM, (the psychiatrist's bible for diagnoses), I stumbled upon an explanation from Eckhart Tolle that rang true. He recalled his own inner struggle while contemplating suicide and quoted the exact words Bob wrote in his suicide letter, "I can no longer live with myself." Eckhart realized there were two competing voices in his head which led him to understand the *I* was his spirit, and the *self* was his ego. The *I* was his true self while the *self,* that he could no longer live with, was his false self.

Upon reading this, it became clear to me that Bob stopped living from his true self and allowed his ego to take over. When I first met Bob, he was passionate, authentic, and filled with inner peace and light. During those last few years, I witnessed the man I married become a partner I no longer recognized. While he had always enjoyed the simple things in life, he became restless and was constantly striving for more money, possessions, and status, all of which he never seemed to have enough. This continued and led to a secret life of gambling and girlfriends.

This aha moment prompted me to learn everything I could about the ego and the influence it had on Bob's death. I learned the ego isn't just the definition of someone who is full of themselves, but it is the fear-based voice at the root of our psychological suffering. It tells us we are not good enough or have enough. It thrives on judgement and negativity while it tries to bury the truth of who we truly are.

The more I learned, the more I became motivated to understand how the ego operated in my own mind. If I understood how to manage my ego, would it be possible to rid myself of negative and self-defeating thoughts? Accomplishing this feat would be a game changer because I'm a believer that my thoughts determine my choices, actions, and ultimately the direction my life will take. If I were to live my best life, I would have to learn the nature of my ego and how to recognize it when it shows up. Perhaps then I could learn to ignore it or shut it down.

While learning to tame the voice of my ego, I trusted the voice of my spirit, which told me to turn Bob's tragic death into something positive. While listening to this voice, I founded Eddy House, https://eddyhouse.org, a nationally recognized center for homeless and at-risk youth to find safety and hope.

INTRODUCTION

Throughout this book, I openly share the dialogue I had between my ego and spirit as I navigated the challenges of creating Eddy House. I also share the many volunteer experiences I had around the world, (a hospice in Tanzania, Syrian refugee camps in Greece, poverty-stricken schools in Ghana, and a blue zone in Costa Rica) where I witnessed the collective ego and collective spirit at play.

I end with an intimate *Tuesdays with Morrie* description of my final days spent with my sister Michele, as she was dying of pancreatic cancer in 2019. I dedicate this book to her.

I have tried to write my story honestly and from the depths of my spirit. I am hoping you will find some aspect of what I have learned to help uncover your own true voice and discover the beauty of who you really are.

The steps to personal transformation and living a life of authenticity and inner peace can be found within these pages. You hold the power to diminish the voice of the ego and tune into the voice of the spirit. It is simply a choice and the choice is up to you.

PART ONE

WHEN LIFE HITS YOU HARD

CHAPTER ONE

MY ORDINARY INSTANT

"Life's challenges are not supposed to paralyze you, they're supposed to help you discover who you are."

BERNICE JOHNSON REAGON

I was unpacking the dishes in our new apartment when my cell phone rang. My husband Bob and I had just moved to San Diego a few days before. It was Rhonda, his secretary, wondering if I knew where he was. I told her my husband had just left to go golfing, and I expected him back around dinner time. She told me, with panic in her voice, that she'd just received an email from Bob. He wrote, "By the time you get this email I will be gone. Please keep the wolves away from my wife. They can no longer chew on me."

I had a dry taste in my mouth and suddenly felt dizzy. She said she was afraid he was planning to end his life, and I needed to find him immediately. I hung up and started calling him. There was no answer. I ran next door to my sister's apartment and banged on her door. When she answered, I blurted out what Rhonda had just told me. Michele tried to calm me down. She assured me, "Take a deep breath and we will figure this out." Michele and I went back to my apartment, desperately trying to make sense of it all.

I called the police. Two officers showed up five minutes later and attentively listened to my story. They asked me what Bob and I had talked about before he left, and how long he'd been gone. One of the officers called the police dispatcher and put in a possible suicide alert with a description of his car. They said they would wait twenty-four hours before putting an alert out to the San Diego media.

Before the officers left, they instructed us to let them know immediately if we heard from Bob. A few minutes later, my son Tim and his girlfriend Hannah, who had been visiting, walked in the door. They'd just finished a long bike ride and were in their usual jovial moods. When I told them about Rhonda's phone call and that we needed to find him, they were silent for a moment. They then began thinking of ways to trace him through his cell phone, or at least we might learn where he'd been via his most recent calls or texts. Tim called our cell carrier, and after explaining the situation to a supervisor, we gained access to his cell phone activity. He found the last message Bob sent. It was to an unfamiliar number in San Diego and said, "Goodbye, I love you." This message hadn't been sent to me. I sat there, stunned. I knew the message was sent to a girl Bob had had an affair with the year before. I thought it was over, but apparently not. Michele also knew about the affair and said, "He must have texted that girl."

Tim looked at me, confused. Hannah sat quietly, her eyes wide open, at the growing drama. I disclosed to Tim that his dad had had an affair a year ago and I assumed it was over. Tim replied he knew something was going on with us but figured we'd worked it out. He didn't want details but added that given the seriousness of the situation, we would need to contact her. My entire body tensed up as he texted her. He informed her Bob was missing and asked whether she knew where he was. She replied, "I'm sorry but I don't know anything."

We sat in the living room trying to piece together where he could be. He had mentioned he was planning to play golf, so we drove around to different golf courses hoping to spot his car but didn't have any luck.

For the next two agonizing days, we heard nothing. We stayed close to the apartment. I kept imagining that he would walk through the door at any time with a smile on his face and a reasonable explanation. On the second night, I was sitting at the kitchen table while Michele was making us sandwiches. I turned on the news. It felt surreal to watch the missing person alert.

At some point, Michele had contacted our older sister, Andrea, and broke the news of what was taking place. Andrea immediately left her home in San Jose, Mexico, and flew to San Diego. On the afternoon of the third day, we were all sitting in the kitchen when my cell phone rang. The caller identified herself as a nurse from San Diego Sharp Memorial Hospital. She said that Bob had just been admitted to the ICU and asked me to come immediately.

* * *

I felt nauseous, and my body began to tremble as I entered the hospital room. Bob lay in the bed unconscious. His arms were heavily bandaged from his hands to his elbows, and he was covered with multiple blankets. His thin body was hooked up to several machines, and he looked pale and drawn, as if he aged years in only a few days. A strap connected his exposed chest to a machine next to his bed and gave off a high-pitched sound. Another machine had plastic tubes attached to his neck and chest. A paralyzing fear began to wash over me. Two nurses were adjusting and monitoring the machines. When they saw me, they stopped what they were doing and one of them came over and gave me a hug. She said there was not much more they could do to save him. Although I was in a state of shock, I managed to get a grip on myself. One of the nurses told me that a hiker had found Bob face down and unconscious in a remote lake east of San Diego. His wrists were cut, and his body temperature was low from having been submerged in the cold water.

That night as I sat by the bed and held his hand, I tried to convince myself that the nurses were wrong and that he would pull out of it. For a moment, I felt hopeful when I saw him barely open his eyes. I could see that he looked confused at first. I assured him that I was there and that he was going to be all right. His look of confusion changed to one of panic. A tear rolled down his cheek and he lost consciousness again. I now know that look of dread was his sudden realization that his attempt to end his life hadn't been successful.

As I continued to sit there, the deafening silence was replaced by the hum of activity in the halls. New nurses came in and introduced themselves as the familiar nurses began to leave. I could see a new day beginning as the sunlight streamed through the windows and I left Bob's side to use the restroom. As I was returning to his room, the sound system clicked on and a man bellowed, "Code blue, code blue!" When I got back to Bob's room, frantic nurses and doctors were scrambling around adjusting the machines, while a doctor was performing CPR. I stood by the door paralyzed, as I watched the doctor trying to resuscitate him. The doctors and nurses were calling out medical terms that I didn't understand. The doctor ceased his efforts after about ten minutes and walked over to me. He explained there was nothing more he could do and that was the moment Bob left this life.

* * *

I got back to the apartment around 8 p.m., and my cell phone rang. The person on the other end identified himself as a representative from the organ donation bank. He apologized for calling so soon after Bob's death but the request and contract to donate his organs had to be done within twenty-four hours. He told me the call would be recorded and I would have to say, "I accept," after listening to him read the contract, which I did. It was late by the time I finished the call and fell into bed. Finally, I could allow myself to cry.

Tim and Hannah were exhausted in the next room resting on the couch. Tim had been voiceless while he tried to process the sudden reality that his dad was gone. Hannah quietly came into my room and crawled into bed with me and benevolently put her arms around me. The gift of love and compassion in that moment is something I will never forget. In *Magical Thinking*, Joan Didion describes the moment her husband died this way: "Life changes in the instant. The ordinary instant." This was my ordinary instant.

MATCHING THREADS

The year was 1973. I was twenty years old with a three-year-old daughter, working as a waitress in the college town of Amherst, Massachusetts, and about to meet the love of my life. Late one night while I was working the third shift at the local diner, he walked in and sat at the bar. He was tall, with beautiful thick long blonde hair that fell to the middle of his back. He had a beard to match, and a sparkle in his crystal blue eyes. I waited on him, and we talked most of the night between my serving other customers. I felt an energy that caused my heart to race and open wide. His name was Bob.

Bob attended the University of Massachusetts and was taking advantage of the benefit of free tuition and expenses that were offered to vets through the GI bill. He had been drafted into the army right after high school and spent two years patrolling the Berlin Wall. He was majoring in philosophy and economics. His home was in Worcester, Massachusetts, where his mother and brother still lived. His father died of a heart attack when Bob was very young, which forced him to work from the age of thirteen to help support the family.

Bob became a regular and always sat in my section, where our conversations continued every night. He usually brought his philosophy books with him because he liked to study the ancient writing of Greek philosophers like Plato and Socrates. He introduced me to their teachings as well as the principles of Stoicism. I became open to a world of new ideas and concepts I had never realized before.

A few days after our first encounter, he asked me over to the house he shared with four other roommates. We spent the afternoon listening to the Grateful Dead while getting to know each other better. We soon became a couple and were together whenever we had the chance.

NEW FAMILY

In the spring of 1974, we moved into our own apartment near the university. My daughter, Jessica, started kindergarten, Bob continued studying economics and philosophy, and I enrolled in the hotel and restaurant management program at UMass. We knew this relationship was going to be long-term and began planning our future together.

On February 14th, 1975, we were married in the Officer's Club at Westover Air Force base where my father was stationed. My father was happy about this wedding. He enjoyed the occasional times when I brought Jessica and Bob by the house for a visit, which was usually on a holiday. Bob and my dad often got into political and philosophical discussions that sometimes became heated and would usually end late.

My father was a military-supporting Republican, and Bob was a peace-loving liberal. The Vietnam War was ending, and Nixon had started his second term. They would argue about our participation in the war as well as the strengths and weaknesses of capitalism. Although Bob would end up sounding like a socialist and my father a fascist, they found common ground when discussing philosophy. They learned that their values aligned when they had discussions about the moral and ethical teachings of Aristotle and other philosophers. Bob became the son my father never had, and my father became the father Bob never had.

The cultural tension at that time was on display at our wedding ceremony. Long-haired hippy friends took over parts of the club, while tight-assed officers and generals gathered to eat, drink, and socialize. When it came time for the club to close, Bob kept the party going by inviting our friends back to our apartment. Joints and shots were plentiful, which may be the reason Bob passed out on the front lawn, only to be woken by the mailman the next morning. Soon after we married, Bob began the process to adopt Jessica. He was always the grown-up in our relationship and felt the adoption would provide stability for all of us, something new to me.

Three years had passed since I'd seen or spoken with Jessica's father, Ron. My not asking for child support had kept him quiet and distant, but now I needed his signature on the adoption papers. I called him and after an awkward catch-up conversation, he agreed to sign everything. I assumed he knew if he refused, he could be hit with a lot of back child support payments.

Our new family spent most of our free time camping and hiking in places I had never envisioned. Bob knew of secret lakes in Maine, Vermont, and New Hampshire. One summer, he took us on an eighty-mile backpacking adventure on the Appalachian Trail. When we could get the time off from school or work, we would visit friends who bought property in parts of Maine and lived off the land.

Two years after we were married, and still in school, we bought a thirty-acre piece of land near a friend's property in central Maine where we planned to someday build a log home and grow our own food. While we weren't sure how we would make a living, we loved the concept of a simple lifestyle. One night, while camping on the land and sitting around the campfire, I remember Bob asking, "Are we spirits having a human experience or are we humans having a spiritual experience?" I looked up at the stars and wondered.

SELLING OUT

As it came time for each of us to graduate with our bachelor's degrees, my father introduced Bob to a friend who was a successful stockbroker. He offered Bob an apprenticeship job in Boston, which would ensure that Bob would eventually get his license to become a stockbroker. Looking back, I see this was a pivotal point in our life. We had to choose between living a simple life in Maine with a community of like-minded friends or jumping into potentially high-powered careers in Boston. We gave into the illusion of the American dream, which paints a picture that happiness can be bought. You need a lot of money from a good-paying job to live the good life. Bob cut his beautiful blond hair. I started wearing a bra and gave up my Moosewood cookbook for fast food. At the same time, disco and cocaine were replacing the Grateful Dead and LSD. It was the beginning of the eighties.

We moved to a suburb of Boston in the summer of 1982. Bob became a stockbroker for a firm in the city, and I was hired at Harvard's Kennedy School of Government as the events and food service director. Once we were established in our jobs, we decided to expand our family and had two more children. Brian and Tim were born a year apart while we both continued to work.

My job involved hosting receptions and dinners for dignitaries from all over the world. I would plan and host events for world leaders and famous guests like Jackie Onassis and John Kennedy Jr. Many of the dignitaries were there to give a speech or participate in a panel discussion that would be televised worldwide. The assemblies and dinners that I oversaw were exciting but entailed a grueling work schedule. I was rarely home. Bob was moving up in the firm, but at the expense of giving up his time with the family. Our time was spent passing the kids off to childcare and working on weekends, while rarely finding space for peace or any kind of gratification.

MOUNTAIN LIFE

On a warm autumn day, we each took a break from work and met for a picnic lunch by the Charles River. We were successful in our careers, but miserable. We were in our mid-thirties and reflecting on where our life was heading. We asked the question, "What are we doing?" We were so in sync in those days, and I truly felt we shared everything including our thoughts and emotions. Our threads wove together perfectly.

We began brainstorming on ways to change course. By this time, Jessica had graduated from high school and moved to Northern California with her boyfriend, Roger. We'd recently taken a trip to visit them in Sacramento and loved everything about the area. After that lunch by the river, we decided to make a bold move. We quit our jobs, packed everything in a U-Haul, and headed west. We made a new home in Roseville, California, where Bob found a job at a brokerage firm. Brian was four years old, and Tim had just turned three, when this new life easily came together.

Bob continued to work as a stockbroker, but never worked on weekends and was home by 4 p.m. every day. I became a legitimate stay-at-home mom with a part-time job teaching aerobics at the local community center. Bob coached each boy's Little League teams, while I joined the PTA and helped in their classrooms. We spent our weekends camping and hiking around Lake Tahoe, where we eventually bought a cabin. We loved soaking up every season that Tahoe had to offer, and eventually sold our home in Roseville and moved to the Tahoe mountain town of Truckee. Bob began his own financial consulting business and worked out of the house. I volunteered at the hospice and worked as a personal trainer at a local recreation center.

I enjoyed my life in the mountains surrounded by the best of Mother Nature. The pristine mountains and lakes awakened a sense of awe and stillness in my soul that made me feel at home. Whenever I had the chance, I would take off hiking and explore the endless trails, creeks, and Alpine lakes with my yellow lab, Otis. I felt aligned with the universe, and everything was perfect. I should have known that life isn't supposed to make you happy and satisfied. It's supposed to challenge you. Little did I know, I would soon meet the toughest challenge of my life.

THE ANATOMY OF GRIEF

Losing Bob forced me to learn about grief, but even today I find the experience hard, if not impossible to describe. It's a hurt like no other, an ongoing kick to the gut suffered inside a dark sadness that sucks all hope and energy out of you. It fucking hurts. The Mayo Clinic describes aspects of grief as numbness, detachment, and a feeling that life holds no meaning or purpose.[1] JK Rowling wrote in *Harry Potter*

---

[1] Sparks, Dana, "Grief; It's complicated," Mayo Clinic News Network, July 14, 2021, https://newsnetwork.mayoclinic.org/discussion/grief-its-complicated/.

and the Order of the Phoenix, "You feel as though you will bleed to death with the pain of it."

    I was no stranger to death. I had lost both parents and several friends over time. I had also done hospice work and facilitated grief support groups over the years, so I considered myself to be an expert on the subject. Now, I know there are no real experts. This abyss felt so deep that I wasn't sure if I could ever climb out of it. Surrendering to it almost felt comforting. I had witnessed others check out of life after the loss of a partner and hadn't understood how someone could become so numb to life. Now, I got it and felt the temptation to give up and simply say, "I'm done."

    The poet and author William Hannan described the feeling accurately when he wrote, "Sometimes all you can do is lie in bed and hope to fall asleep before you fall apart." It was a struggle to fall asleep but when I did, the hollow feeling in my chest and lump in my throat would return as soon I woke up. I would realize this was real and not a bad dream. The tears would come in a sorrowful rage because I couldn't make sense of it all. I knew I was in a dark place, but a calm and comforting voice emerged from my spirit and told me I would be okay.

* * *

Spirit is defined as a force within a human being thought to give the body life, energy, and power.[2] The spirit is that familiar part of you that is your solid core throughout your entire life. While all the cells in your body replace themselves and life situations change, the spirit remains the same. It is who you really are. It has also been described with words like consciousness, soul, inner being, and our higher self.

---

2 *Merriam-Webster.com Dictionary,* s.v. "spirit," accessed October 23, 2022, https://www.merriam-webster.com/dictionary/spirit.

We can get a sense of our spirit in the stillness of watching a sunset, looking up at the stars, or in the present moment. The Japanese poet, Izumi Shikibu wrote, "Watching the moon at dawn, solitary, mid-sky, I knew myself completely, and no part left out."[3] Words try to describe spirit, but you must experience it before you truly know it. It's like telling someone what chocolate is. But you really don't know what chocolate is unless you taste it. It is something you feel with a deep sense of knowing. Your true essence. The formless dimension that is deeper than our thoughts or our mind. Deepak Chopra describes the soul as "The core of your being. It is the eternal reference point that you should always be in touch with."[4] It is that solid inner strength and knowing that gives us hope to push through anything that life may throw at us.

* * *

As the days and weeks passed following Bob's death, the voice from my spirit showed up more and more. It said, "Hold on girl, yes this sucks big time, but you're strong enough to get through it. You are more than what happens to you. Remember this and breathe." As I listened to this voice, I could feel the dread and darkness gradually dissipate to a calm stillness and acceptance.

My ability to tap into my spirit was the result of years of practicing and studying spirituality. I was trying to find the answers to all the big questions that we ask ourselves, like what is this thing called "life" all about, and what are we supposed to do with it? My spiritual journey had begun years before when I began meditating and immersed

---

3   *The ink dark moon: Love Poems by Ono no Komachi and Izumi Shikabu, Women of the Ancient Court of Japan.* 1990, Vintage Classics.
4   Chopra, Deepak, *The Seven Spiritual Laws of Success: A Practical Guide to the Fulfillment of Your Dreams.* Chapter One: The Law of Pure Potentiality. 1994, *New World Library.*

myself in books that attempted to answer these questions. Books like *The Power of Now* by Eckhart Tolle and *A Course in Miracles* scribed by Helen Schucman stirred up so many thoughts and feelings about my own existence and helped me realize that I had more control over my destiny than I thought I had. They spoke about the true essence of spirit we all have within. Now my spirit was being seriously challenged.

CHAPTER TWO

MOTHERLESS CHILD

I was nine years old when my mother died. Ours had been a normal military family living in different places around the country that included California, Georgia, Texas, and Massachusetts. I was continuously forced to adjust to new schools and friends. During our move to McCoy Air Force base in Florida, my mother came down with what she thought was the flu. The movers met us at our new home and unloaded the truck. The boxes were never unpacked. Instead, my mother stayed in bed and rarely left her room.

Two months later she went to the base hospital. I wasn't allowed to see her, because in those days children weren't permitted inside, even to visit a relative. On a random day, one that would become one of those game-changer days, my father called my two sisters and me into the living room and told us that our mother had died. The flu had turned out to be breast cancer.

The loss of my thirty-four-year-old mother was also the loss of my childhood innocence. She greeted my sisters and me each morning in the kitchen with a warm hug while she prepared our breakfast. The kitchen was usually filled with the smell of freshly baked cinnamon rolls and the sound of jazz playing from her favorite radio station. If I had a nightmare, she never hesitated to let me crawl into bed with her and my father. She took pride in dressing her three daughters in clothes she meticulously sewed herself. After her death, I no longer felt a solid foundation beneath me. My sisters and I were basically on our own. Andrea, the oldest sister, had just turned fourteen. Michele, being the youngest, was eight.

My father struggled to maintain his position as a Lt. Colonel. He was a radar navigator on the B52 bomber, and went on numerous round-the-clock flight missions, which usually took him away from home for three to ten days at a time. We were left on our own during his absence. When he was home, he would go into his room and shut the door, and although he was across the hall and his door was closed, I could hear the faint sound of him weeping in the middle of the night.

In the weeks immediately following my mother's death, our neighbors living on the base would stop by with casseroles and baked items and linger in the house while talking with each other. It felt awkward to have these strangers coming in and out. Michele and I spent most of the time hiding out in the bedroom we shared. Andrea had struck up a friendship with a girl who lived next door. They were gone most of the time meeting other friends they had on the base.

Eventually, the neighbors and food stopped coming and soon the cupboards were empty. Michele and I ate what was served in the school cafeteria, thinking lunch might be it for the rest of the day. When my father was home between missions he would go to the base commissary and load up with boxes of Corn Flakes and cartons of milk. He would also come back with cans of Spam, which always made me gag after I opened them. The milk would be gone after a couple of days, and then our meals consisted of bowls of dry cereal. I never ate the Spam no matter how hungry I felt. I wore the same unkempt clothes every day and rarely took a bath. Andrea woke Michele and me up for school each morning, but no one checked us out as we left the house. I'm sure we looked like unsupervised children.

MOVING ON

Two weeks after my mother's death, my father made arrangements for her funeral. It was held in Duluth, Minnesota, which was considered "home" to my parents and where our extended family lived. It was also the place where I was born and had lived for the first year of my life. The service took place on a chilly and overcast day in November 1961. The trees were bare and the sidewalk leading to the church entrance was covered with leaves. My sisters and I sat together in one of the front pews of the church. My mother lay in the casket placed by the altar. When the pastor finished talking, my sisters and I were told to walk in single file next to the casket for a last look at her. She was so still and looked asleep. Her dark hair contrasted with the pasty, off-white color of her round face. She was dressed in the special blue and white outfit that she usually only wore to church. My father must have picked it out, believing it to be appropriate. She also had three red roses placed on the center of her chest. Someone thought they would be a nice touch, each rose representing the three of us girls. I saw Andrea touch Mom's cheek, and she later told me that her face felt hard like cement.

After a couple more days of sitting in someone's kitchen surrounded by strangers, casseroles, and cakes, we flew back to Florida to our silent home filled with those same boxes that still needed unpacking.

The unpacked boxes remained scattered across the living room for a few more months. Then one day my father told us that he had arranged for us to move back to where we had previously lived in Springfield, Massachusetts. My father requested the transfer because he thought it would be best if we went back to our familiar schools. Trying to deal with losing his wife and now tasked with raising three daughters so foreign to him, was too much. He needed help.

We stayed with family friends for a few months until he rented a house that was to become our new home. The house was run down and dingy inside. It felt empty and uncomfortable even though the movers had filled it with our familiar furniture. From the day we moved in, my sisters and I were convinced it was haunted. Creaky noises came up from the basement and mysterious shadows seemed to move on the walls by the narrow staircase that led to the attic.

It was the middle of January when I had to go back to a new fifth-grade classroom. There were a few familiar faces, but there was no one that I considered to be a "friend." I felt different and out of place, from the first day back. I could hear the whispers of curiosity and felt the blank stares from my classmates. The first week of May, the art teacher assigned Mother's Day cards to the class, which made me feel anxious and embarrassed. While the teacher passed out construction paper, crayons, and markers, I could hear the quiet comments and snickers from a couple of the girls near my table wondering what I would do with mine. I reluctantly put something together, and when it was time to take it home, for no one, I threw it in the trash barrel outside of the door.

I didn't like school, and soon my sisters and I realized that we didn't have to go because my father was away on military assignments for weeks at a time. He designated Andrea, who was fifteen by now, to be in charge and gave her money for food. We would spend it on candy, bus fare, and tickets for the midnight shows at a downtown theater. Movies like *Psycho* and *Brides of Dracula* kept us paralyzed in our seats while munching on popcorn. The principal of our school finally caught on to our exploits and set up a meeting with my father to encourage him to step up his supervision, but that didn't happen. He was numb to the whole idea of suddenly becoming a single dad.

TESTING THE LIMITS

I started eighth grade in September 1965. I was mostly a loner, except for Michele, who was a year behind me. I could count on her to meet me in the hallways or in the girl's room to smoke one of the Viceroy cigarettes that we'd lifted from my father's packs, which were usually left on the kitchen counter.

Michele and I were sisters, best friends, and reliable accomplices. We depended on each other for everything as we tried to navigate the loss of our mother, as well as the freedom we now had. We covered for each other if our father or the school asked too many questions about our grades or where we were. I was an expert at forging my father's slightly slanted signature on a variety of notes sent to and from our teachers. I signed a few of our report cards that required a parent's signature. My father never asked to see a report card and would have blown up if he saw our dismal grades. I tried to avoid the tirades that caused his face to turn scarlet red and his voice to get loud enough to shake the house.

If we decided to cut school, I also wrote our absence notes. We would occasionally make that decision while waiting at the bus stop for the school bus. This bus stop accommodated both the city busses and the school busses. Many times, it was the first one that showed up that determined which one we got on. Michele and I were so in sync that all it took was a certain look or nod between us to make the snap decision. If we took the city bus, we would get off at the downtown stop. We would duck into the Woolworths record store and look through the stacks of singles and albums from bands like the Beach Boys or the Miracles. When we were ready to move on, we would head to the nearby park to smoke a cigarette.

FINDING OUR TRIBE

One sunny and crisp fall day, we recognized a group of boys from our school who were also skipping school. They were huddled together around a park bench and passing around a bottle of Bali Hai wine wrapped in a paper bag. They saw us smoking our Viceroys and called out to come over and join them. As the day went on, we realized we had found our tribe with these misfits.

I was particularly interested in the one who had a mischievous grin and seemed older than his age of fourteen. His name was Danny, and he stood at least four inches taller than the others. He looked a little mysterious with his deep-set eyes and crooked smile. He spoke with confidence and seemed to find everything amusing. He told us about an unlocked janitor's closet on the second floor of the school that was a good place to sneak a cigarette. He also had us all cracking up when he told us how he snuck into the teacher's lounge and put dog poop in their refrigerator without getting caught.

One day while Michele and I were taking the bus home from school, we noticed Danny and the others in a car behind the bus, honking and waving. Danny was driving and motioned us to get off and join their joy ride. Earlier that day at school, the boys told us they had stolen a car the night before and had parked it on a side street near the school. Although we knew this must be the stolen car, Michele and I looked at each other and simultaneously called out to the bus driver to stop. We jumped off the bus, and after climbing into the back seat, were off to the local gravel pit where Danny spun the car around, doing donuts and crazy eights while we all shrieked with laughter.

We started meeting the boys after school and on weekends in a wooded area next to a vacant lot that we called "the spot." We made campfires, smoked, and drank whatever any of us could steal from our parent's liquor supply. Michele and I pulled from my father's Cutty

Sark and vodka stash but then replenished the bottles with water thinking he wouldn't notice. One bitterly cold night after hanging out at the spot, we quietly snuck in through the back door hoping to not wake our father. We thought we were in the clear, until he flipped the kitchen light on. He was sitting at the table with a Cutty Sark bottle in front of him. The only thing he said was, "You both are grounded for a week." Then he went to bed. I remember feeling slightly guilty for the trouble we caused but not enough to change my ways. We were back at the campfire the next night.

One night, Danny told me his parents had died in a car crash the year before and the state had placed him in a foster home. We began to spend more time together between classes at school and at our hangout in the woods, where he gave me my first kissing lesson. I expected this kiss to feel awkward and mechanical, but it felt natural and effortless. I felt a mesmerizing attraction and closeness between us that I had never felt with anyone before. His foster parents knew that he was spending time with me and invited me over for dinner. I was nervous when his foster parents picked me up and brought me to their home. Danny and I sat in the backseat as I awkwardly responded to their attempts to make conversation. When we arrived at their home, Danny gave me a tour of the house.

The small, two-storied, gray cedar-shingled home was furnished with traditional oak furniture and felt orderly, clean, and uncluttered. Danny showed me his room, which was upstairs and at the end of a hall. We sat on his bed and while working on our kissing skills, his foster father suddenly opened the door. His face froze, and after a long pause, he ordered us to go downstairs for a serious discussion. I felt a little embarrassed, but Danny reacted as though he thought the whole situation was funny. He told his foster father to relax as he grabbed my hand and led me to the living room. His foster father reminded me of my own defeated father. He seemed flustered and overwhelmed because he didn't know how to deal with unruly adolescents. He sat in front of us and after scolding us, for what seemed like at least an hour, he told Danny that he was not a good fit at their home and would be calling social services to let them know. Early the next morning before his foster parents woke up, Danny packed up his few possessions and hitchhiked downtown where he rented a room in a boarding house.

He wasn't in school the next day and I wondered if social services had moved him to another school. He called me the next night and told me that he was kicked out of the boarding house after getting into a fight with another guest and had nowhere to go. I felt a desperate need to be with Danny and to figure this situation out together. I told him he could sneak into our basement and sleep on the couch next to the washing machine. That night, I made sure the latch on the basement door was undone. I dozed in my bed until I heard a rock pinging against my bedroom window. I snuck downstairs, past my father's room, to get down to the basement to welcome my overnight guest.

This went on for at least a week until Danny was picked up by social services. They had been searching for him since he'd left the foster home and never went back to school. They let him call me before they shipped him off to a home in another state. Danny was my first love and first heartbreak.

I missed Danny but his loss didn't slow down my search for a good time. Michele and I continued to meet the others at "the spot," but one night, we brought our party to the home of one of our friends. Her name was Karen and she lived in our neighborhood just down the street. She told us to be quiet as she let us come into the unfinished basement where we all sat on the cement floor and passed around cigarettes and whatever alcohol we had. As the night went on, we all got a little drunk and rowdy. The boys began to swing on the exposed electrical wires hanging from the ceiling until sparks shot off, and the power went out. We became quiet and sat there in the dark until we heard steps coming down the stairs. We were blinded by the flashlights aimed at our faces. That's when I realized my father had been upstairs visiting with Karen's father and was now furiously shining a flashlight at Michele and me.

NEW RULES

My father realized he'd lost control of us. At least that's what my sisters and I assumed because he went on a search for a wife or someone to supervise us when he was away. He had the added pressure of filling this position soon, knowing he was about to be stationed in Guam. He had been assigned to participate in bombing raids over Vietnam and would be gone for a minimum of six months.

One Saturday afternoon, he woke Michele and me up (we slept until noon or later whenever we could) and introduced us to Barbara. She was in her twenties, petite, and barely said a word. She was a secretary at a local bank, single, and living with her mother, and about to become our stepmother. I'm not sure if she knew at that time what she would be facing. I was fifteen and Michele was almost fourteen. We were used to making our own decisions and were not about to give up our freedom and independence. We rarely saw her again during the two months that passed from her introduction to the day of their wedding.

Right after Barbara and my father were married, he left for Guam to fight the war, and left Barbara with the responsibility of keeping us out of trouble. It soon became clear that she would be fighting a war of her own while living with the enemy. She asked us to do chores around the house and we'd just scoff at her and tell her she couldn't tell us what to do because she wasn't our mother. We added that she was just a hired maid my father married. Yes, we were bad. Looking back, it must have been lonely and overwhelming for her to try and manage this dysfunctional household on her own.

In the fall of 1967, Andrea moved out and married her boyfriend Joe, soon after realizing she was pregnant. Joe had recently signed up for the military and was stationed at the same base where my father worked. They met through friends and started dating, which led to acts of bravery when Joe would climb up a tree near our house, hop on the roof, and climb through Andrea's window to secretly spend the night.

ALTERNATIVE PERSPECTIVES

My wild spirit continued in high school when Michele and I, who were veteran pot smokers by then, became introduced to LSD. It wasn't unusual for us to meet our friends before school, drop acid, and then go to class. I remember an experience in my "girls math" class when I was fixated on the teacher. She taught all of us girls, whom she assumed were to be future homemakers, how to use math to shop for our future families. If a dozen eggs cost one dollar, what would six eggs cost? As I sat at my desk and the acid kicked in, I watched her move her mouth, but the sound of the words was coming from her right ear, which appeared to be a talking cauliflower.

The Vietnam War was still raging at the time, and friends in our group were starting to receive the dreaded draft notice. Some followed the instructions to show up, some fled to Canada, and some, like my friend Paul, got creative. A couple of weeks after Paul got his notice, he shot off his baby toe to get a medical exemption. Michele and I ran into him at a rock concert not long after the incident. He was grinning from ear to ear while he told us that losing his toe was his ticket out of going and most likely not coming back from Vietnam. "Who needs a baby toe anyway?" he said, while we passed a joint around.

On the last day of my junior year, Michele and I left home. It was the early summer of 1968 when we hitchhiked to Cape Cod, with no plan other than to get out of Springfield in search of an adventure. I'm sure Barbara and my father found peace in our absence. Barbara had just given birth to a baby girl, Melanie, and they were adjusting to becoming new parents. For three months, we partied and got high while picking up occasional short-term waitressing jobs to get us by when our resources ran thin. We didn't have a place to stay so we spent many nights sleeping on the beach in Provincetown. After we were kicked off the beach, we found an inconspicuous place to sleep in the local cemetery, off the cop's radar. I went shoeless from June until September, except for the cheap flip-flops I wore while waitressing. By the time summer was over, I could walk on broken glass and crush out joints and cigarettes with my bare feet, a skill I was very proud of.

When September arrived, we reluctantly returned to school. Michele and I spent most of our time hanging out at a friend's apartment after class, getting high, and listening to music. I was seventeen and Michele had just turned sixteen. On Halloween night, while we passed pipes around and listened to the Velvet Underground, someone said there was a concert downtown. Michele and I were always up for anything, so after popping some orange sunshine (LSD), we headed out in hopes of finding live music.

We arrived at the municipal auditorium a short time after the band started playing their first set. The doors were wide open, and no one was checking tickets, so we snuck into the back area. I immediately felt myself melt into the music as the sunshine kicked in. I glanced over at Michele who looked like a blonde bohemian gypsy as she danced barefoot in the aisle. The entire building was visibly vibrating with sounds I had never heard before. I felt as though I were being lifted to the ceiling by a beautiful and powerful voice that went right through me along with the soul-touching sounds of drums and guitars. We stayed to the end and left dazed and euphoric. The next day we learned this random band was called Led Zeppelin.

THE FIGHT INSIDE

LIFE IS A PARTY

Michele and I remained single because we liked it that way. We were having so much fun on our own without the rules and restrictions that always come with relationships. However, in my senior year of high school, that changed when I became attracted to one of the guys in our hippy tribe. His name was Ted, and he was the crazy and fun one in the group. He had his own car, a Volkswagen Bug with peace signs painted across the hood. His good looks and easy-going personality drew everyone in, including me. We became a couple, and the group threw a huge party when we were married.

The wedding took place at a friend's house that welcomed at least fifty young hippies who we considered to be one family. The house was filled with pot smoke, and people danced until the sun came up to the music of the band playing in the living room. The Justice of the Peace was a white-haired elderly man with a large glass eye who was obviously uncomfortable and sped up the blah-blah-blah so he could collect his twenty dollars and leave. Most everyone at the party, including Ted and me, eventually found a couch or space on the floor to catch some sleep as the drugs wore off and the sun came up. Michele and I drove home together the next morning in a spaced-out daze recalling all the craziness that just transpired. We walked into the house and went directly up to our room without having to answer any annoying questions from Barbara.

I met up with Ted a couple of days later. It was awkward, as we had never really thought about what would happen next. It was one of those "oh shit" moments for me, but he was good with the idea of us being married, each living at home with our parents, none the wiser. He never took anything too seriously or thought past tomorrow. I, on the other hand, felt as though my free spirit was becoming caged and knew that I screwed up.

Michele helped me find a cheap lawyer to draw up annulment

papers, but there was a catch. Because I was a minor, I would need my father's signature. It seemed crazy to me that you could get married at sixteen without parental consent, but you couldn't end it on your own unless you were eighteen or older. The lawyer knew I wanted to keep my father clueless, so he suggested I have Andrea sign on behalf of my father, and the lawyer would tell the court that he was "incapacitated." Andrea reluctantly accepted the task because she knew the potential blow-up that this would cause at home. It eventually worked out. Ted was accommodating and life rolled on.

NEW FRIEND

High school graduation was coming up, and Michele and I expanded our tribe to include a couple of senior guys from our school. I became attracted to the quiet one named Ron, who had a bad-boy edge to him. He was not like most of my friends who were on the wild side. Ron pretty much kept to himself and was considered "straight," meaning he didn't do drugs.

One night, Michele and I asked our new friends to meet us at a dive bar that we occasionally frequented, and where they never checked IDs. We met them there and found a booth in the corner where we ordered beers. I had a few squares of blotter acid with me and asked them if they wanted to try it. Ron hesitated at first but then out of curiosity he joined in. We sat in the corner drinking our beers and goofing around until we all got quiet as our perceptions changed. Ron and I danced to the music of Jimmy Hendrix and The Doors that played on the jukebox. We talked and danced until the lights came on and the bar was closing, and then we went home.

That first "date" led to Ron and me spending more time together. He lived on the second floor of a semi-shabby tenement building with his parents and older brother, Ivan, on Foster Street, in the sketchy part of town. His parents had immigrated from Russia when Ivan was a baby and settled in Springfield. Ron was born soon after his father found a job as a machinist in a local factory. Ron's father saved up his earnings and eventually bought the two-story tenement house and rented out the first floor. His parents didn't speak English, and Ivan had such a strong accent that he was difficult to understand. Ron invited me over one day after school when his parents weren't home. It was like walking into an ancient Russian thrift shop. There were doilies hanging over the tattered furniture, and heavy tapestries covering most of the walls. Ron showed me where he slept in an overstuffed, thread-worn chair across from the couch where Ivan slept. The only bedroom in the home was reserved for his parents.

As time went on, Ron and I spent more and more time together, which led to contortionism in the back seat of my car. A few months went by, and I realized that my period was late. I was also feeling off and nauseous in the mornings. I was seventeen and pregnant. A child about to have a child.

TIME TO GROW UP

The thought of becoming a mother was beyond my comprehension. I knew that I was not fit, prepared, or willing to take on that responsibility. I had just graduated from high school. I had no vision of my future, but I knew being a mom was not what I wanted.

As time passed, it was harder to hide my baby bump. I finally told my father. He had had a similar conversation with Andrea when she'd told him she was pregnant, but she had a plan and a boyfriend. I hadn't even told Ron and had no plan other than I wasn't ready to become a mom. His solution was to instruct Barbara to find me a doctor and take it from there. She made an appointment and after the exam, the doctor pronounced to me, "You better grow up fast because you are about to have a baby." Apparently, I was about six months along.

I told Ron and we agreed the only solution was to get married and become parents. He had a job in a garage fixing cars, and I was waitressing, so we saw ourselves as financially secure. We asked his parents if we could rent the attic apartment of their house, which we did. It was up three narrow flights of stairs and had been empty for years.

Michele arranged for a modest wedding to take place in the three-room apartment that was about to become my new home. She hired a Justice of the Peace and invited my father and Barbara along with Andrea and Joe and a few friends. My father refused to come at first, but at the last minute, he changed his mind and showed up. Michele and I were shocked when we realized the JP was the same one who'd officiated at my wedding with Ted only ten months earlier. We nervously squirmed while he performed his duty hoping he wouldn't remember or say anything. While this man officiated the nuptials, he looked bewildered, and I'm sure he remembered me, but fortunately, he didn't say a word. We had the required paperwork and his payment. That was all that mattered.

Ron, Michele, and I pieced together secondhand furniture Michele had found in a thrift shop. We crammed a slightly used crib into the pantry space in the kitchen that was to be the baby's room. Within a few nights after moving in, I went into labor and Ron drove me to the hospital. He asked me if I wanted him to come in or just drop me off. I asked him to come in with me, which he reluctantly did, but he was gone by the time our daughter was born. She was nine pounds and twenty inches long. A small amount of light-colored hair was matted down around her tiny red face. She wiggled around in my arms after the nurse wrapped her up in a blanket and carefully handed her to me. An unfamiliar feeling of love and connection washed over me. I named her Jessica.

THE FIGHT INSIDE

REALITY ISN'T ALWAYS FUN

The first year with Ron was miserable and bleak. It was a challenge living in the same house as Ron's family, even though they lived downstairs. I was alone most of the day tending to Jessica, while Ron worked at the garage. Strong smells of cabbage and borscht permeated the entire house, and the sound of Russian opera music blared constantly. I could also hear his parents getting into heated arguments regularly. Sometimes it would end with yelling and screaming followed by intense banging on the walls that sounded as if things had gotten violent. I told Ron how the fighting made me anxious and afraid to be home, but he told me to relax. I looked forward to the three nights a week when I went to my waitress job at a local diner.

It was not uncommon for Ivan to go on drinking binges that usually led to fits of anger, so I did my best to avoid him. One night while Ivan was downstairs drinking and getting into a heated argument with his father, I heard gunshots. I grabbed Jessica and jumped up onto the bed, thinking it was the safest place if the shots went through the ceiling. I could see Ron was terrified of his brother and afraid to intervene during Ivan's bouts of rage and drinking.

I loathed being married, but as time went on, I grew into the role of being a mother. Michele was a huge help, but that ended when she went away to nursing school in Minnesota. I felt lost without her while I cared for Jessica during the day, then went to my waitress job three nights a week.

As time passed, Ron began to lose his temper over the pettiest things. One day while we were driving in the car, without any warning, he backhanded me across my face. I remember the impact of it and the hurt that followed. He accused me of looking at a guy who was standing on the sidewalk. I sat there stunned and tried to hold back the tears. Could this life on Foster Street in Springfield get any worse?

I was nineteen and had one friend, who happened to be a neighbor. We would occasionally see each other when I was out walking Jessica and stopped to chat about things going on in the neighborhood. She was also married, so one day I decided to confide in her about Ron hitting me. I confessed how I felt shame and confusion about being treated this way and didn't know what to think. She shrugged it off and replied, "This is just what husbands do. It's normal and we just have to deal with it." This was 1970 and a time in our culture when women kept quiet about domestic violence. There were no safe houses or support systems, and it was assumed that family affairs should be kept private. I let it go.

I counted the days until Michele would be home on her winter break from school. The day finally came, and she couldn't wait to catch up and see how much Jessica had grown. Ron was in the apartment when she showed up and kept to himself while Michele and I hugged and talked, until he interrupted and said he wanted to speak to me in the bedroom. He shut the door after I walked in and backhanded me again. Apparently, he was insulted because I wasn't paying enough attention to him. Michele heard me cry out and barged into the room like a crazed grizzly. I don't remember exactly what Michele said or threatened him with, but I do remember Ron telling her it was none of her business, before abruptly storming out of the apartment.

The next day, Michele came back when she knew Ron would be at work. She told me she had a friend, Sandy, who was moving into an apartment and was looking for a roommate. This was my chance to get Jessica, who was now two years old, and myself out of this abusive home. I had been secretly stashing a portion of my tips over the past few months with the desperate hope that a way out would somehow magically appear.

Michele arranged for Sandy to meet me at the apartment where we could figure out the logistics and finances of becoming roommates.

A few days later, while Ron was at work, I gathered my clothes and Jessica's things, packed it all in my compact Datsun, and left that house on Foster Street, forever. When Ron saw that I had gone, he immediately called Michele. She said he sounded furious when he asked her where we were, but she kept my whereabouts a secret.

FREEDOM

Things fell into place. I picked up a couple of extra waitressing shifts at the diner and made arrangements with a babysitter to watch Jessica. I felt emancipated. A few months passed and I started a new job at a local pub-type restaurant that guaranteed better tips and more hours.

This is where I met Tom. He was well above average height with a muscular build and had shiny long dark hair pulled back in a ponytail. He lived in Amherst, a small progressive college town east of Springfield, and happened to be in town visiting a friend. He sat at the bar and when I took his order, he started a conversation by asking my name. It was a slow night, so we talked on and off between the few customers that came in. When he paid his bill, he asked for my number, and when he called the next day, we made plans to meet on my upcoming day off. He picked Jessica and me up and took us to Amherst and showed us around town, and the commune where he lived.

I felt like I was in a foreign land as he introduced me to this place they called "Happy Valley" with five colleges all within a few miles of each other. This college town had magnificent tree-lined streets, eclectic shops, restaurants, and bars everywhere. Amherst felt alive and full of color, opposite from the dismal black and grey that I was used to in Springfield.

The commune consisted of a nine-room farmhouse with an attached barn surrounded by a few acres of open land. Chickens and cats roamed freely on the wrap-around front porch, the main gathering place for the fifteen residents. Inside the farmhouse, there were several bedrooms and makeshift common areas.

While Tom introduced me to his roommates, I was thinking, these people live the way they want, on their own terms. This is what I want. Everyone had migrated there to enjoy a simple and laid-back lifestyle that centered around sharing with others. Conflicts were settled over an honest discussion and the passing of a joint. Some worked odd jobs while others made crafts they sold on the sidewalks in town. I met a couple who were musicians and played in the local bars. They had a four-year-old daughter, Daisy, who introduced herself to Jessica while Tom showed me where he lived, inside the barn. He had built a bed and makeshift closet in one of the corners close to where he kept his motorcycle.

Jessica had just turned three years old. She was brimming with curiosity and loved the word "why." She was always content wherever I took her. I dressed her in denim overalls and made a ponytail out of her curly strawberry-blonde hair. She resembled me but had Ron's hazel eyes.

It wasn't long before Tom asked me to move into the barn with him. He built a bed for Jessica and made room for me. I was excited to move in, but first I needed the approval of the others who lived there. Mark and Susan, who organized everything around the house, called a meeting to vote on whether my daughter and I would be allowed to join the commune. Everyone met in the spacious kitchen and voted yes. I agreed that I would pay the usual $35 a month for my space in the barn, and pitch in with household duties. I was also required to work in the co-op once a month and pick up the weekly bread order at the day-old bakery thrift shop.

I gave Sandy notice, and after quitting my Springfield job, I picked up a couple of waitress jobs in Amherst. My new roommates at the commune said they would watch Jessica while I worked. It was a perfect set up!

THE FIGHT INSIDE

Cutting my ties with my prior life meant that I had to get a divorce from Ron, whom I hadn't heard from since I'd left six months earlier. I went to a legal assistance office where they charged a minimal rate to put together the official papers and scheduled a date for Ron and me to appear before a judge. I showed up at the courthouse, but Ron wasn't there. I waited for my turn to stand in front of the judge, who asked me what I wanted for child support. I told him I wanted nothing and could raise Jessica alone. He looked annoyed with me and said that while I didn't seem concerned enough for my child's welfare, he was. He set an amount of $60 a month that Ron would be required to pay. I wanted to leave Ron and my past behind, so I found the court clerk and asked him not to send the court's notice for payments to Ron. He said it was his job to serve these notices, but he would see what he could do. I never received a payment from Ron or heard back from the court.

I always looked forward to spending time with Tom. His laidback personality and drama-free life made it feel natural and easy to be around him. I also fit in with the rest of my roommates. While Jessica and Daisy played together in the yard, we all helped with feeding the chickens and keeping up with the garden. Someone was always playing a guitar or harmonica on the front porch. My new home was filled with good vibes.

Tom and a couple of other roommates tended an area behind the barn, where they grew and sold a good amount of marijuana. Tom expanded his interest from selling pot to only friends to becoming involved with large-scale distribution. He had a cousin in Boston who was selling pounds of pot, which was more lucrative than selling the mere "lids" or ounces that came from the backyard garden. Tom eventually partnered with his cousin, and they began selling all over Happy Valley. This business venture made everyone in the house a little nervous, including me, when Tom would welcome "business acquaintances" over to the house for drop-offs and pickups.

I knew what he was doing was illegal, and I didn't want to be involved in any way. Motherhood had lowered my risk level. I also felt a lack of privacy with strangers coming into my space in the barn at all times of the day or night, so I told Tom it had to stop. He said it was a temporary arrangement and would end soon, but it didn't. Whenever I brought it up, he would snap at me and tell me it was none of my concern. It became apparent that my needs or opinions didn't matter to him any longer. I started sleeping with Jessica in her bed and distanced myself from Tom whenever he was around. The joking and laughter were replaced with a cold silence. It wasn't long before he packed his things and moved to Boston. I was glad to have the barn to myself.

Two months later, I would meet Bob at that all-night diner and my life would change again.

CHAPTER THREE

LIFE IN TRUCKEE

After Bob and I, along with our two sons, moved to Truckee in 2003, I became involved with the local hospice. I wasn't sure if I had the aptitude for it, but I felt drawn to volunteer. Bob encouraged me to always challenge myself and supported the idea of volunteering when I had the time and desire. I was nervous going to my first assignment even though I had successfully completed six weeks of training that focused on the mental and physical stages of the dying process.

MARY

My first patient was an elderly woman named Mary who lived by herself and whose only companion was a scruffy-looking pound dog named Bear. Although she had terminal lung cancer, and was confined to her bed, she smiled and spoke with a calm and kind voice when I was first introduced to her. I asked her to tell me stories about her life in Tahoe as a single woman who worked as a power lineman. Her eyes lit up as she told me tales of being the first woman allowed on the team who would repair the power lines during dangerous weather conditions. She recalled stories of climbing telephone poles in the middle of the night during blizzards and taking on risky jobs that her teammates were too afraid to do.

I soon developed a daily routine with Mary. It began with taking Bear for a walk and then sitting by her bed and conversing with her about whatever came up. I also helped with chores around the house while a nurse tended to Mary's hygiene needs or adjusted her pain meds. After about two weeks, Mary began to talk less and sleep more. She occasionally woke up but seemed dazed. I continued to sit with her while she slept and applied a cream to her dry lips and slipped ice chips into her mouth. Her sister traveled from Montana to see Mary, and the day after her arrival, Mary passed. I later learned that it wasn't uncommon for hospice patients to die right after visiting with a loved one whom they hadn't seen for a while. It's as though Mary purposely held on until she had a chance to say goodbye to her sister.

I felt humbled and honored to be present with Mary at the end of her life's journey, as her spirit passed through the veil. I knew then that I loved this work because it gave me the opportunity to connect with others in a way that is raw, real, and honest.

It's unfortunate that our culture has a fear and denial about death. Although we know we all die, we don't want to talk about it. A study found that two-thirds of those surveyed did not have an advanced directive in place and felt uncomfortable talking about their death.[5] There is a "conversation disconnect" when it comes to talking about death. While 90 percent of Americans know they should express what they would want at the end of life, only 30 percent do.[6] The

---

5 "Majority of Marylanders Without Advance Medical Directives," John Hopkins, February 17, 2010, https://publichealth.jhu.edu/2010/pollack-advance-directive.

6 "Conversation Disconnect," The Conversation Project, September 18, 2013, https://theconversationproject.org/press-release-first-national-survey-on-end-of-life-conversations/.

French Philosopher, Charles de Montesquieu thought that we had it backwards in the way we think of birth and death. He said, "There should be weeping at a man's birth, not at his death. Life is hard and death says, 'Congratulations, you made it and now it's time to move on.'" Being present at someone's passing has felt to me like attending the ultimate graduation ceremony.

MARIA

My next assignment was to work with a fourteen-year-old girl named Maria, who was suffering from osteosarcoma, a form of bone cancer. Maria had been living in Reno, Nevada with her mother and younger brother. Maria's mother had come to Reno after illegally crossing the Mexican border a few years before Maria was born. Unfortunately, Maria's mother got involved in drugs and prostitution while living on and off the streets with Maria and her brother. Eventually, her mother was arrested and deported to Mexico, and the state placed Maria with her aunt and cousins who lived near Truckee.

Soon after Maria moved in with her aunt, she began having pains in her leg which led to the diagnosis of osteosarcoma. The doctors didn't know exactly how long she would live but assumed it would be less than a year. Despite the heaviness of her problems, she tried her best to live just like a normal teenager. She went to school between chemo treatments and never complained about the pain.

I taught her how to drive my car, which turned out to be her favorite thing to do. She didn't have a license, but I sensed that when she was present and focused on driving, her mind escaped the fear and anxiety that lived in her head. The cancer grew, and the doctors decided it was necessary to remove her leg. I continued to let her drive with only one. Many would have judged me as irresponsible, but I didn't care. It was worth it to see the happy look on her face.

I accompanied Maria to her many doctor appointments and treatments where she hoped the doctors would leave her with some good news, but none did. I talked to the doctors about the possibility of experimental treatments but was told Maria would not be a candidate because there was already a list of people waiting who could afford the outrageous costs. I was also with her when hospice came and set up a hospital bed in her room, which I knew would be the bed she would die in. She passed through the veil a week later.

CALLS FOR HELP

I expanded the scope of my volunteer work and joined the Disaster Action Team of the Red Cross. On Halloween night, 2006, shortly after I completed the training, there was a horrific fire in downtown Reno. A woman had set a mattress on fire in the hallway of the historic Mizpah Hotel. Twelve people perished. My job was to interview the survivors and offer help and resources after they'd lost everything in the fire.

One seventy-year-old woman told me how she and many others fled their rooms, crawling on the floor of the dark hallway, in search of a door or window. She said she desperately moved as quickly as she could, while there was screaming and chaos closing in behind her, but then it suddenly stopped. At that moment, she knew the fire had reached her, which made her even more desperate to escape. She frantically found a window and managed to open it before she climbed out and jumped the two stories to the ground. I heard many more stories like that and felt as though I was helping these people just by listening while they processed what had just happened.

My next Red Cross assignment took me to San Diego to help victims of the Southern California fires of 2008. Three major fires destroyed at least 400 houses and 500 mobile homes. I went out with a team to help those who had lost their homes and possessions in the fire. Again, I learned that a valuable way to help was to simply listen.

THREADS UNRAVELING

Life in Truckee seemed perfect, but as time went on, Bob became more restless and distant for reasons I didn't understand. Instead of spending an afternoon by the lake or finding undiscovered trails to explore together, he would stay in his office upstairs with the door closed. We began drifting apart, seeing less and less of each other as he traveled more and more.

He formed a close relationship with an attorney who became his new business partner. They worked with a team who specialized in complex financial transactions. I noticed the distant change coming over Bob soon after he started working and traveling with this group.

Bob wouldn't talk much about what they were involved in, telling me that I wouldn't understand. He had always tried to keep work and family separate, but I became more curious when he began getting official-looking letters from the Justice Department. He told me he and his partners were being sued, but it was nothing to worry about, and their attorneys were handling it. I let it go and didn't think much more about it, even though legal notices continued to show up in the mailbox.

One day, while picking up the mail, I was surprised to find a letter from the Dean of the Social Work Department at the University of Nevada notifying me that I had been accepted into the program as a graduate student. Bob had encouraged me to apply because he knew how much I enjoyed helping people and that is what social workers did. I also knew from my work with hospice that if I had a degree, I could do a lot more. The social workers were allowed to work with the nurses and patients on a deeper level of care. I wanted that.

THE FIGHT INSIDE

I was excited and nervous when I started my first semester in the fall of 2007. It was an adjustment to keep up with my classes and the house while continuing to do my volunteer work. With this new schedule, it was apparent that Bob and I had less time together, and when we were together, he continued to seem distracted.

On New Year's Eve, I planned a quiet and romantic evening at home for the two of us. I picked up appetizers at the local gourmet shop and made his favorite Italian dish. I wanted our limited time together to be special, and a chance to reconnect and catch up. He had been traveling over the weekend and was due home in the early evening. He told me that he was at a client meeting in Iowa and would be home around 4 p.m. It was close to 2 p.m. when a recorded call came to the house phone from an airline saying his flight from San Diego would be postponed due to heavy fog. This baffled me at first because he said he was in Iowa, but then I realized he was lying about where he was. I panicked and began to understand that because of this and other changes in his behavior, he was most likely having an affair. I anxiously sat and waited to hear from him as the night went on while trying to convince myself there would be a reasonable explanation. The airline must have made a mistake.

He finally called much later and sounded agitated and defensive. He attempted to explain the call with a story that didn't make sense. After I pressed him for the truth, he admitted he had lied and was actually stuck in San Diego after visiting a woman he had been seeing for a while.

I could barely hold the phone, shaking and choking back tears. When I hung up, I collapsed. Bob and I had been soul mates, lovers, and best friends for thirty-four years, and now I didn't know who he was. I began questioning my sanity and my life while asking myself if I couldn't trust Bob, how could I trust anything or know anything in this world to be true ever again? I felt lost, confused, alone, and shattered. Our lives would never be the same.

LIFE IN TRUCKEE

SEARCHING FOR TRUTH

He came home the next day. We couldn't escape the reality of what happened and knew we needed to talk. My emotions were all over the place, so I took the time to let them settle. I knew from my therapy courses that my anger and confusion had to stay out of everything. It would only get in the way of trying to get to the truth. He started by saying that he had been unhappy and stressed out from work and also felt a lost sense of purpose with the kids growing up and moving out on their own. He continued by saying that the affair had put a spark back into his life, even though he knew it was wrong in every way. I calmly listened as if I were outside of my body, while inside I was trying to keep it together long enough to allow him to tell the whole truth.

He met her the year before in a bar in Las Vegas. She was twenty-eight years old and an aspiring model. They started meeting whenever he had business in Las Vegas. He said these meetings made him feel alive again. He then said he felt a deep sense of guilt and would end it immediately.

While I sat there and listened, so many questions raced through my mind. Is this a mid-life thing he is going through? Have I been too complacent in our relationship? Have I been giving him enough attention? Somehow the anger was gone, and I started feeling like this was my fault for not making more of an effort to keep the spark going in our relationship, especially while the boys were launching out of the house. I didn't know what to think.

The next few days felt like walking on thin ice and at any time everything could crack wide open and fall apart. These were days of silence and thoughts of what next. I found an excuse to go out when I knew he would be home. I tried to make polite conversation over dinner. The air was saturated with tension. I passed through the victim phase, and when the anger was gone, I began to realize this wasn't about me but something dark and sad was going on with the person I loved. I didn't understand it. We talked more about his unhappiness, and he agreed with me that seeing a therapist might help. The next day I helped him find one, and about two weeks later, he went to his first session. He said talking with this therapist helped him to think about things from his childhood that he never thought about before. He was going once a week, but that was all he would say about the sessions.

A couple of months went by, and we tried to get past the affair by pretending nothing happened. But everything was different. I planned special date nights and made an extra effort to dress up and be attentive, only to have him spend our time together on his cell phone talking to someone about business and looking for distractions to avoid being present with me. We were both miserable and not sure what to do with our lives, but we knew this wasn't working and we had to make a change.

One Sunday morning while we were sitting at the kitchen table, I told him I needed him to be honest with me and tell me exactly what was going on. I told him I couldn't live with the silence and tension I felt between us any longer. He listened and opened up, telling me about the stress he felt from his work and the lawsuit. He said while he didn't do anything illegal, he felt that he was used by his partners to oversee business transactions that were close to unethical. Bob had a reputation for his high principles and was known as a straight shooter and a solid guy. He said he couldn't trust his business partners any longer and was planning to cut ties with them.

He also told me our finances had taken a huge hit with the recession that had consumed the country. He had made poor investment decisions over the past few months, and we were behind on the mortgage with little hope of catching up. He said we owed more on the mortgage than what the house was worth. Bob always handled our finances, which had been fine by me, but looking back, I should have been more involved. He also said he felt miserable living in the isolation and cold weather of Truckee. Although the weekly counseling sessions he had gone to for the past three months helped somewhat, he didn't find them useful any longer.

He knew he needed a change in his life, so we both agreed we were ready for a new path forward and formulated a plan that we believed would promise a brighter future. This is similar to the conversation we had years earlier in Boston before the move west, but this one seemed more desperate.

NEW HOPE

We decided to leave the house to the bank and move to balmy San Diego where he would work as a golf marshal on a golf course, which had always been his dream job. I would somehow figure out a way to finish my last year of graduate school. The plan seemed to bring life back into him and our relationship. We packed everything up and with the help of Tim and Hannah, we moved to San Diego. We rented an apartment on the island of Coronado, in the same complex where Michele lived. Life felt good and full of hope for the first time in a long while.

On the second night after we arrived and spent the day unpacking and getting settled into our new place, we all took a break and went out for dinner. I had never seen Bob so relaxed and at peace with himself. We had a wonderful evening, and he was present with each of us. While we walked back to the apartment, he stopped and gave me a hug and kiss that will forever be tattooed in my mind. He said he was proud of me and thought I was smart and strong. He added how he would pretend to understand some of the academic papers I wrote and asked him to proofread, but the content was over his head. Looking back, I can see that he was trying to prepare me for what was to come. We went to bed that night, and while I watched him sleep peacefully, I thought to myself that I finally have my guy back. What I didn't know was that he would be gone the next day . . . forever. We had breakfast together the next morning before he left to golf, and I could never have imagined that the next time I would see him would be in the hospital where he left us all on May 17th, 2010.

CHAPTER FOUR

PROCESSING

For weeks after Bob's death, I sat in the apartment and stared at the remaining unpacked boxes feeling numb. I called Jessica the day after he died and told her what had just happened. She listened and after a long silence, broke into tears. In her disbelief, she kept asking, "Why?" and I kept saying, "I don't know." I also called Brian, who had just gotten home from his job in Truckee. He screamed, "NO," into the phone and then asked the same question that Jessica asked, "Why?" He said he would make plans to come to San Diego and told me, "We will get through this."

Tim and Hannah went to get Bob's car, which he'd left at the scene where he attempted to end his life. When Tim started the engine, Grateful Dead music blared from the speakers. They also found his golf clubs in the trunk, which was not unusual, except they were covered with fresh grass. Bob must have played his last game of golf just before he walked into the lake.

I kept thinking of the email he sent to Rhonda. His message, "Keep the wolves away from my wife, they can no longer chew on me," kept playing in my head. It seemed that his connection with these business partners influenced his decision to take such a drastic step. I felt I had to let them know they played a role in Bob's decision, so I sat down and wrote the following email to every business associate that I could find in Bob's contact list.

> *Bob is gone. He was collateral damage in your world of manipulation, betrayal, backstabbing, and greed. Maybe this is a time for reflection on how our actions have consequences on others and that it's not about money and power but about how we treat each other along the way. In his final goodbye, he said he found comfort in knowing, "They can no longer chew on me." Bob is finally at peace.*

Perhaps I was looking for a way to vent my anger and confusion, but I did hear back from some who said they felt my message was powerful and certain individuals deserved to hear it.

Soon after I sent this email, I had a text from "the girlfriend." The text read, "Before I start the process, we need to talk." I took a deep breath as the voice from my spirit appeared. This voice told me that no matter how crazy things get, I would be fine. It recalled a quote I once read from *A Course in Miracles*, scribed by Helen Schucman that said, "Nothing Real Can be Threatened." My spirit was real and couldn't be harmed. My spirit would protect me from anything life threw at me. It told me to step back and witness this movie as though I were sitting in the audience, rather than as an actor on stage in this dark drama. Inhale. Exhale.

My first reaction was to text her back to find out what she meant. Is she pregnant? What could she want from me? But then I thought, what good could come out of pursuing this? I responded to her text, "Do not contact me again. You mean nothing to me." That was the end of it, but I wondered about their relationship and have many questions that will never be answered.

I went through Bob's bank records and found numerous charges from high-end stores like Gucci, Cartier, and Louis Vuitton along with

PROCESSING

room and cash charges at Las Vegas resorts. These charges ranged from a couple of hundred dollars to a few thousand dollars each. The one that hit me the hardest was for two nights at the Ventana Inn at Big Sur, which sits dramatically on a cliff overlooking the Pacific Ocean. It was a place we used to pass when we took the boys camping. We always dreamt of staying there someday. The date of the charge was the same date as our last anniversary, which Bob said he had to miss because of a business trip. I probably should have felt enraged, but I didn't. I missed him.

I knew I had to call Bob's mother, Pat, but wasn't sure what I would tell her. She lived in Hyannis, Massachusetts, at a senior living apartment complex. She was deeply religious and made a point to walk the two blocks from her home each day to attend the morning service at the Catholic church. I finally called her, but I couldn't manage to tell her the truth about Bob's death. I knew telling her Bob was gone would be hard for her to process but knowing he died by suicide would be an even bigger blow. I told her he suddenly had a heart attack just like his father had years earlier. She was silent for a couple of minutes and then let out a gasp of denial. She said, "No, this can't be!" I asked her if she would be alright and suggested I could fly out to be with her. She assured me that she would be fine, but I wasn't so sure.

I called the church she attended and asked to speak with a priest. After being put on hold, a man answered and introduced himself as Father Johnson. I explained that I had just left Bob's mother with tragic news about her son, and I asked if he would stop by her apartment to check on her and perhaps console her. He explained that he was very busy but could take the time if I agreed to send a donation to the church. His request gave me pause because although Pat lived on social security and the occasional checks we sent her, she always managed to leave an offering at each service she attended over the past twenty years. I reluctantly made the donation.

THE FIGHT INSIDE

I wasn't sure what my future would look like. The boxes were still packed and piled high in the living room. Rather than unpack them, I felt an immediate need to get involved with something sane and meaningful. Something real and good to focus on. I had been spending too many bleak days in the dark. Two months after Bob's death, I began to volunteer at a youth homeless shelter in downtown San Diego. My job was to provide an adult presence and offer assistance to the stray kids who randomly showed up. I also accompanied the outreach team to the homeless camps set up along the seawall at Ocean Beach. We passed out basic supplies and resource information to the youth who were living there. Again, I learned the value of listening. Two months later, I decided to leave San Diego and return to Truckee and finish school. The kids gave me hugs and thanked me on my last day at the shelter. I wanted to tell them, "No, thank you!" They had no idea how much more they gave me than I gave them.

RETURN TO RENO

Michele and I drove the 600 miles back to Truckee with Bob's ashes in the back seat. I knew the house on Stallion Way was eventually going into foreclosure, but I figured I could stay there until the bank locked it up. Bob had taken out a life insurance policy years ago that would be enough to live on but not enough to keep the house. Soon after we were back, Brian, Tim, Hannah, Michele, and I climbed Martis Peak, which overlooks Lake Tahoe, and scattered Bob's ashes on the forest floor under a grove of tall pines. I put aside a scant portion for my own personal memorial to him that I later spread beside a creek and near a trail Bob and I had hiked many times together. It was a place where we sat and meditated while soaking up the stillness and sounds of the forest. I have visited that spot on his birthday ever since.

PROCESSING

Staying in the house felt empty and lonely with all the reminders of Bob everywhere. His brown leather jacket hung on the coat rack, where he had left it. Late one night, a stranger rang the doorbell and said he was looking for someone in the neighborhood and wondered if I could help him. He asked me my name during the conversation and when I answered, he pushed an envelope into my hands and said, "You have been served. Have a good night." He turned and hastily got in his car and drove off. I remember standing on the porch in the dark feeling depleted, and without even opening the envelope, I went to bed. The next morning, I opened the envelope and read the letter. It said because I was Bob's wife, I was recognized in a lawsuit and all our assets could be seized. This must be what Bob meant about "keeping the wolves away from my wife."

A few days later as I walked to my car after class, I received a call from Paul White who said he had been Bob's attorney and a friend. He believed Bob was innocent in this lawsuit and explained to me what it was about. The suit claimed that Bob oversaw and allowed one of his business partners to take funds from a company that the partner wasn't entitled to. This attorney offered to represent me free of charge. I accepted and thanked him for his generosity.

Paul set up a four-way conference call with the attorneys who filed the suit. I didn't know what to expect when the call began, but I was taken by surprise by aggressive threats and accusations. I asked them what they wanted from me. I told them everything was gone, and the house was in foreclosure. I asked them if they wanted Bob's leather jacket that was left hanging on the coat rack. I told them I didn't understand what this was all about, but I knew Bob had integrity and wouldn't have done anything wrong. Although I wanted to believe what I was saying, I wasn't sure. I wasn't sure about anything anymore. A couple of hours after the phone call, Paul called and said they had removed me from the lawsuit.

The bank had started to foreclose, and soon I would be locked out of the house, so I looked for a place to live in Reno. The money from Bob's life insurance policy allowed me to buy a two-bedroom condo downtown, close to school. I didn't want to take anything with me from the house except my clothes. This was a similar move that I made when I left Foster Street many years earlier. It was time to put the past behind me.

Summer was coming to an end, and I was ready to return to school and finish my master's degree in social work. Returning to school also meant reuniting with my classmates and colleagues in the department. My friends talked about traveling and spending time with family over the summer break. They asked me how my summer vacation was. It was a struggle to manage my emotions when I told them Bob died by suicide, but I knew I was among compassionate peers who were good listeners.

DIAGNOSIS

Everyone, including myself, assumed Bob must have been clinically depressed. After spending some time studying the DSM, psychiatry's bible used to diagnose patients with mental illness and personality disorders, I wasn't so sure. Bob didn't fit the basic criteria for a depressive disorder. While he did show signs of increased anxiety and detachment, he didn't have a loss of appetite, sleep disturbances, lethargy, or diminished cognitive ability. I thought about asking his therapist to help me figure out what had been going on, but knew it was against the same code of ethics that I, as a new social worker, would be bound to uphold.

After trying to diagnose, label, and classify the mental factors that caused Bob to take his life, I knew in my gut it simply was a matter of him giving up his spirit. He stopped listening to his inner voice.

PROCESSING

I first recognized this during the last few years of his life. I could see that he was becoming someone who, at times, I didn't recognize. He became more consumed with his business and seemed to always be searching for distractions and ways to avoid being still. He became restless, anxious, and constantly looked for new things to buy or ways to expand his business. He was obsessed with gaining status and recognition, believing that is what it's all about. He never seemed to have or do enough, which was not the Bob I once knew. The Bob I knew was compassionate, thoughtful, and someone who appreciated nature and the small pleasures in life.

We used to hike and take time to sit in the forest and meditate together. I remember the last time we did this. He couldn't sit still for more than a couple of minutes before he was ready to head back. Eckhart Tolle writes, "When you lose touch with your inner stillness you lose touch with yourself. When you lose touch with yourself, you lose touch with the world." I remember asking Bob at one point, "Do you own the mask or does the mask own you?" He looked at me without answering, then walked away. I could tell by the stunned look on his face and his inability to answer this question, that the mask had won.

A year before he took his life, I gave him a copy of *The True Men of Old*, which I had read years ago written by the ancient Chinese Philosopher, Chuang Tzu.[7] I told him I was worried that he was moving away from his true values. He knew what I meant but ignored what I was trying to tell him. I understood that the girlfriend, secrets, and lies were an attempt to fill the empty inner void he felt with temporary pleasures as his spirit weakened. The same copy of *"The True Men of Old"* that I had given him a year earlier was one of two things left in his briefcase on the day of his death. It read:

---

7 Chuang Tzu, "The True Men of Old" *The Writings of Chuang Tzu*: Book 6, www.nothingistic.org.

"What is meant by a 'true man?' The true men of old were not afraid when they stood alone in their views. No great exploits. If we can free ourselves of the striving to be someone special, to be a certain way, or to have certain things—free of that desire to be or to do or to have anything at all—we can relax into the natural unfolding of the Dharma."

The other thing left in his briefcase was an envelope addressed to me. It included a letter that said he made the choice to end his life and wished that I would respect that decision and he loved me. I struggled with his request to "respect his decision" as I could see and feel the devastation that his choice left me and the rest of our family. The last sentence that Bob wrote in his goodbye letter said, "I can't live with myself any longer. I have chosen the Existential approach. It is my life and I have chosen to end it." I am forever finding it hard to accept that ultimately it was his journey and that his choice to end it should be treated with acceptance and respect. I'm not sure I'll ever get there.

WHAT THE FUCK HAPPENED?

As the days passed, I tried to imagine what could have been going on in Bob's mind before he took his life. This question kept nagging at me until one day when I happened to be reading *The Power of Now* by Eckhart Tolle. In the introduction, he told how he experienced many years of depression and was on the brink of suicide. He said to himself, "I can no longer live with myself." He described how he examined this thought and asked the question, "Am I one or two?" If I cannot live with myself, there must be two of me: the "I" and the "myself" that I cannot live with. He thought, "Maybe only one of them is real." He found peace with the realization that the "I" was his true self witnessing the unhappy and deeply fearful false self that was at the root of his negative thoughts. He began to only listen to the voice of his true self and eventually, the voice of his false self became silent. He described this false self as his ego. *I cannot live with myself any longer.* Wait, what? These were the exact words Bob wrote in his suicide letter. I put down the book and wondered, "Is this what happened to Bob?"

Looking back, it was clear that Bob's spirit (the **I** that Eckhart spoke of) shrank as his ego (the **self** that Eckhart referenced) grew. When we first met, he listened to the voice coming from his spirit that reflected a sense of contentment and peace. He enjoyed the simple things in life and took time to "smell the roses." The voice was calm and loving. This changed when he began to ignore this voice and listened to the voice coming from his ego. The voice from the ego told him he would find happiness with more money, possessions, and status. While he was still feeling unsatisfied, the voice told him temporary pleasures of girlfriends and gambling would fill this void. Of course, that didn't happen. As time went on, the voice became louder and more negative until it became unbearable. He couldn't live with it any longer.

CHAPTER FIVE

THE VOICE OF THE EGO

In the months following Bob's death, I kept thinking about this concept of the ego or the "false self." What is it? Where did it come from? How could it be so destructive? I started reading everything I could find on the ego, and I became convinced that learning to manage this "false self" may be a way to prevent psychological suffering and discover true peace and happiness. Could it be that simple? I set out on a quest to learn everything I could about the ego and how it operates.

* * *

Ego isn't just the definition of someone who is full of themselves but possesses a more complicated and sinister meaning. It has been described for centuries by philosophers, psychologists, as well as religious and spiritual leaders in different ways. Freud's interpretation included mommy issues and sexual repression, which many feel is outdated and irrelevant.[8] Carl Jung wrote, "The ego wants explanation always in order to assert its existence. Try to live without the ego. Don't allow yourself to be led astray by the ravings of the animus. He will try every stunt to get you out of the realization of the stillness which is truly the self."[9] Ryan Holiday, author of *Ego is the Enemy*, wrote "Ego leads to envy, and it rots the bones of people big and small."[10] Wayne Dyer said, "The ego is only an illusion, but a very influential one. Letting the ego illusion become your identity can prevent you from knowing your true self."

The thoughts of a young child are openhearted and filled with curiosity, wonder, and love. Our caregivers reward and punish our behavior to teach us to conform with the norms of society. As children, we learn to seek their approval and adapt to what is expected of us. Through our thoughts, we begin to fear others and question our abilities. We eventually exchange who we truly are for who we think we should be.

Although the ego does what it can to suppress our true self, it isn't all bad. It can serve as a useful tool to help us interact with the world through our conditioned self or personality. It helps with tasks, planning, job performance, and daily activities. Because the ego knows it's an illusion, it competes with the true self to ensure its existence. This power struggle is where we often mess up. If we let our guard down and turn our authentic power over to the ego, we suffer. This psychological suffering can show up as a sense of isolation, greed, depression, insecurity, shame, guilt, anxiety, resentment, self-doubt, and more. We ultimately live a life that's false and set spirit-denying limits on ourselves. We learn from the ego that if we stay

---

8 "Are Freud and Psychoanalysis Still Relevant?" Alliant, accessed November 15, 2018, https://www.alliant.edu/blog/are-freud-and-psychoanalysis-still-relevant
9 Jung, Carl, *C.G. Jung Letters, Vol. 1: 1906-1950*, Princeton University Press, 1973, pg 427.
10 Holiday, Ryan, *Ego is the Enemy*, Portfolio, 2016, pg 116.

in our comfort zone, we will not be vulnerable to judgment and failure. We usually choose the safe path which can be settling for a mediocre life that doesn't allow us to fully experience joy, freedom, and authenticity.

The more I learned, the more I became motivated to understand how the ego operates in my own mind. If I understood how to manage my ego, would it be possible to rid myself of negative and self-defeating thoughts? Accomplishing this feat would be a game changer because I'm a believer that my thoughts determine my choices, actions, and ultimately the direction that my life will take. It became clear to me that to live my best life, I would have to learn the nature of my ego and how to recognize it when it shows up. Perhaps I could then learn to ignore it or shut it down.

THE EGO IS NOT YOUR AMIGO

The ego doesn't want you to be joyful and satisfied with your life. It's as simple as that. It's a parasite that feeds on negativity and fear to ensure its existence. So don't feed it. Just as darkness cannot survive with light, the ego tries to keep your thoughts fearful and dark while distracting you from the love and light of your spirit. It can be sneaky and hard to spot, but we must remain vigilant to recognize when our thoughts get in its grip. That is when we need to be grounded in our spirit and ignore the ego. While accepting that it is a part of us, our goal is to become the master of the ego rather than it's slave.

Think of the mind as our operating system running two programs, fear (ego) and love (spirit). It is the amount of power and influence coming from either the ego or the spirit that will determine the lens through which we see the world. A perspective of the world as half empty or half full.

OPEN-HEART MINDFULNESS APPROACH®

I'm a visual learner and like to use diagrams to make sense of things. I created a scale I call the Open-Heart Mindfulness Scale to show the effects our thoughts have on our feelings. You can see that it matters where our thoughts are coming from, ego or spirit.

I use this scale as a self-check when I recognize myself slipping into a negative way of thinking. If I find myself on the left side of the

OPEN HEART MINDFULNESS SCALE →

EGO	1	2	3	4	5	6	7	8	9	10	SPIRIT
FEAR											LOVE
NOISE											PRESENCE/PEACE
UNWORTHY											WORTHY
OUT OF BALANCE											ALIGNED
SEPARATE											CONNECTED
DEPRESSION											JOY
WOUNDED											HEALED
MASK/IMAGE											AUTHENTIC
INSECURE											SECURE
RESENTMENT											GRATITUDE
SHAME/GUILT											SELF ACCEPTANCE
SELF DOUBT											CONFIDENCE
SCARCITY											ABUNDANCE
ARROGANCE											HUMBLE
COMFORT ZONE											NO LIMITS
GRIEVANCE											FORGIVENESS
CONTROL/RESIST											ALLOW
STAGNATION											CREATIVITY
LOW ENERGY											ENTHUSIASM
APATHY											COMPASSION
BELIEVE/ASSUME											TRUTH
ANXIETY											CONTENTMENT

scale and immersed in an ego-based mindset, I put my attention on the attributes on the right side. This brings me to a more positive place and better aligned with my spirit. Energy flows where attention goes.

Obviously, we would all like our thoughts to live on the right side of this scale, but that isn't so easy. Remember the ego is sneaky and uses a bag of tricks to pull us to the left. I reached into this bag and pulled out a few of the most common tricks the ego tempts us with. They include identification, comparison, not enough, and beliefs vs. truth. I realized it's impossible to entirely avoid these traps because we are human. I'm sure even the Dalai Lama steps in it from time to time. The key is to make peace with the ego, but don't take it seriously. It's a trickster and should always sit in the passenger seat while you drive the bus.

Another tool I use when my thoughts and emotions are causing me to feel uneasy or negative is the **REAL** method.

- **Recognize** the disturbance. Accept the unpleasant emotion or thought. Sit with it. Don't try to suppress the feeling. What you resist will persist.
- **Examine** the source of the feeling. What trap of the ego are you slipping into? What unhealed wound is triggering this feeling?
- **Acknowledge** with self-compassion from the seat of your spirit.
- **Let it go!**

Now, let's examine the common ego traps of identification, comparison, not enough, and beliefs vs. truth.

IDENTIFICATION

As the ego tries to pull you away from your spirit or true self, it wants you to take on a false identity with concepts that may include your role, status, possessions, job, appearance, etc. You become that role, that status, your possessions, or your appearance. If you lose what you have identified with, you feel destroyed because that is who you think you are. Wayne Dyer stated, "Ego, the false idea of believing that you are what you have or what you do, is a backwards way of assessing and living life."

The ego can also encourage you to find an identity through a religion, political group, gang, or cult. It uses our desire to feel accepted and significant as a way to lose oneself within a particular group. You find yourself stripped of your intellectual and spiritual freedom as you are entirely indoctrinated into this other belief system.

COMPARISON IS THE THIEF OF JOY

We spot our ego showing up every time we judge someone, which basically involves comparing their worthiness to our own. We all catch ourselves doing this. We size people up as either inferior or superior to ourselves, which is a way we measure our value and relevance in a situation. However, the act of comparing ourselves to others gives them the power to determine our own self-worth.

If we feel someone is superior to us, we measure ourselves as less than equal and are left feeling insecure and possibly jealous or envious. Conversely, if we judge someone as inferior to ourselves, we assume we are above them. The ego loves this because it results in either a feeling of self-righteousness or arrogance.

The spirit doesn't care how you measure up against others. It only cares that you are true to yourself because that is all that matters. You accept people for who they are without judgment, expectations, or comparisons. You just do you.

ENOUGH OR NOT ENOUGH

Two of the most common tactics employed by the ego focus on scarcity and striving. Scarcity is the ego's way of telling you that there is never enough. You spend your life striving to have enough or become enough. This goal is impossible to achieve because the ego is aided and abetted by our consumer culture and will convince us that there is always more to acquire or accomplish. This lack of satisfaction can lead to greed and depression because you will realize that no matter what you have or do, it will never feel like enough. There will always be a feeling of emptiness and lack.

Unfortunately, some people go through their entire lives feeling this way. Wholeness and the satisfaction to know that you are enough can only come from the spirit. Corporations hire marketing experts and make billions when they exploit our ego-based beliefs by telling us that we will be envied by others and find happiness if we buy that designer handbag or that fancy car. The spirit knows this is crap and doesn't fall for it. Sure, we may experience superficial moments of happiness there, but it will soon pass, and you will be thinking of the next purchase. Unlike fleeting moments of pleasure, true joy is lasting joy and comes from the spirit and is expressed through a strong sense of knowing that you are enough, just the way you are.

BELIEFS VS. TRUTH

The ego does not like truth because the ego is your false self and thrives on illusion. Truth is the domain of the spirit. It's crazy how fast we can allow any random situation in life to go sideways and cause all kinds of drama in our heads when our thoughts are based on assumptions. Rather than act on an assumption in a way, I would most likely regret, I've learned to objectively think about what is going on and determine what is true and what is not. After deciding what the truth is, I will either do something about it or let it go. The great Stoic philosopher Seneca said, "We suffer more in our imagination than we do in reality." When we are facing a challenge, it's easy to let our imagination go wild and conjure up all the "What ifs?" that will make us crazy and stressed out. The more logical approach would be to figure out and focus on what we can control and let go of what we can't control.

Another name for fear is **f**alse **e**vidence **a**ppearing **r**eal. Remember that the fear-based ego is your false self and will do what it can to keep that illusion going by distorting the truth. The spirit humbly seeks the truth. Many times, it's not about the story but our narrative of the story. Confirmation bias is a term used when we selectively conform facts to fit our beliefs while disregarding the truth. While the ego tries to support a reality based in illusion, the spirit only considers facts to find the truth in a situation. In his farewell address, Barack Obama said, "Increasingly, we become so secure in our bubbles that we accept only information, whether true or not, that fits our opinions, instead of basing our opinions on the evidence that's out there."

WOUNDS LURKING IN THE PSYCHE

Okay, I just told you about the common egoic traps of identification, comparison, not enough, and beliefs vs. truth. Those aren't the only dirty games the ego plays. In fact, the hardest to spot and most dangerous trap is found in the wounds we bury deep in our psyche. Pay close attention to this one. It's a beast!

Often, the past events and relationships in our lives trigger us and need to be examined. Many times, we are triggered because of an unhealed wound that just got poked. We all have them. Ram Dass said, "If you think you are enlightened, go spend a weekend with your family." These wounds stem from raw emotions left over from being bullied, rejected by someone you loved, pressured by overly critical parents, etc. Our thoughts are a reflection on how we *think* about the story. Our emotional reaction to a wound reflects how we *feel* about that unpleasant story from the past. Either way, the negative thoughts and emotions that are oozing from an unhealed wound will lurk around in our psyche and cause mental suffering until we face them honestly and scrub them clean.

Don't try to stuff these feelings because what you resist will persist. The negative feelings that we store inside our psyche build up pressure and cause suffering until we release them. Carl Jung referred to this "shadow" part of us as repressed feelings, concepts, and thoughts we have about ourselves that we don't want to face. The source of these wounds will be uncovered when we embrace the unpleasant feeling rather than avoid it. Each time we honestly face and examine our wounds, we release its energy and lose our identification with it. To get past it, we must go through it, and eventually, it will no longer have power over us. This entails honest and deep self-reflection and is usually not a lot of fun, but it is the only way to heal.

SELF-LOVE

A few years ago, I read an obituary of a teenage boy who had died by suicide. His family said they could see the beauty and love in him but unfortunately, he couldn't see it and didn't love himself. Remember, the ego does not want you to be happy. It wants you to be seriously uncomfortable in your own skin. It flourishes when you feel unworthy, separate, wounded, and filled with guilt and shame.

I have worked with many clients who were filled with self-loathing, and I would ask myself how I could teach them to love themselves. I've learned it is ultimately an inside job. Although counseling can help, it is the individual who must do the hard work to scrub out their wounds. It's like guiding them to the light switch in a dark room, but they have to flip it on. I've also learned that self-forgiveness is the first step toward self-acceptance. Hey, none of us are perfect. We have all done dumb shit. Rather than beat ourselves up about it, we should take responsibility, own, and acknowledge our mistakes, and then move forward. Learning to be compassionate with ourselves is part of our personal growth and spiritual evolution.

* * *

There it is. I just gave you a general description of the ego. The rest of this book will offer examples of how I incorporated what I learned about the ego into my life after Bob passed. You will see that lessons learned from his death created his legacy and shaped my future. I hope you find some of these lessons helpful in shaping your own future. A future lived in spirit.

PART TWO

TURNING A NEGATIVE INTO A POSITIVE

CHAPTER SIX

FUTURE SOCIAL WORKER

"In the depths of winter, I finally learned there is in me an invincible summer."

ALBERT CAMUS

In May 2011, one year after Bob's death, I finally finished school and graduated with my master's degree in social work. During my years working as a volunteer, I always felt limited because I didn't have the right education. I had been apprehensive about going back to school because I hadn't been in a classroom since I earned my bachelor's degree in hotel and restaurant management twenty years earlier and didn't know if I was up for the challenge.

On the second day of my behavioral theories class, I sat in a seat at the front, with my notebook open and pen ready. I looked around the room and saw that everyone else was taking notes on their laptops. I didn't even own one. When the instructor began talking about accessing our coursework on e-campus, and linking up with online study groups, I realized I was in way over my head. Panic settled in as my stomach tightened and I began to sweat.

I got up from my seat and escaped into the hall to find the restroom. I made it into the nearest stall just before unleashing a flood of tears. What was I thinking? After many deep breaths, I pulled myself together, left the restroom, and went back into the room just as the class was ending. I asked the instructor, Mary Hilton, if I could have a few minutes with her. After she finished with the other students, I told her I would be dropping out and thanked her for her time. She half smiled at me, and said she wasn't going to let me give up so quickly and would arrange for support to help me out. I left the building feeling a new sense of hope and motivation. To this day, I am grateful that she saw something in me that I failed to see.

Okay, remember I told you I would show you examples of my ego showing up? Well, that was one. I felt inferior to the other students when I compared myself to them. My spirit recognized my self-doubt and said, "Don't concern yourself with how others are doing. There will always be others who have a higher skillset than you. Focus only on yourself and do your best. You may find you are able to meet this challenge. And if you don't succeed, so what. At least you tried."

I was out of my comfort zone, but the more I stuck with it, the more determined I became to become successful in this world of academia. As I began to get papers and tests back that had As and Bs on them, along with encouraging remarks like, "Great job" or "Well done!" my confidence level grew. I not only enjoyed the classes, but I connected with the other students who, like me, were there to hopefully make a difference in the world.

A sign that hung on a classroom wall read, "I am a Social Worker . . . Refuting social and human injustice. Supporting the right to self-determination and dignity, I dare to fight for the voiceless and disenfranchised. We change lives when we bring action and compassion together. I'm proud to be a social worker. Social Work is not a career. It's who you are." This sign may seem a bit optimistic, but the words tapped into a part of my spirit that sparked an inner knowing that I was in the right place, with the right people, at the right time of my life. It felt as though the deep joy that was hiding out in my inner being, was now aligning with the needs of the world. A perfect fit!

NO JUDGEMENT

Along with classwork, the social work program included two years of internship experience. I was allowed to submit two preferences, but there were no guarantees. My first internship was with an organization that worked with juvenile sex offenders. This had been my first choice, because I wanted a challenge and to engage with teenagers. The program housed boys who had been found guilty of a sexual offense and sent to a locked-down live-in facility. The offenses were non-violent and ranged in seriousness from sexually abusing a young family member to sexual experimentation with a family pet. When the boys completed the program, they were exonerated. More importantly, their names would not appear on the National Sex Offender Registry for the rest of their lives. That was monumental.

 I worked twenty hours a week under the guidance of Dr. Jennifer Moore, the in-house psychiatrist. Her no-nonsense rapport with the kids was offset by her engaging smile and dry sense of humor. She directed me in supervising the boys' daily activities and lessons. I was also responsible for one-on-one case management sessions with five of the thirty boys. On my first day, I was shown around the facility and introduced to the staff and kids. I shadowed Dr. Moore and sat in on a staff meeting that included the counselors and case managers.

They talked about each boy separately and brought up any issues or concerns they had. Common infractions included trying to get out of chores or starting a fight with another boy. They discussed and agreed upon a consequence or a change to their treatment plan, which usually included an adjustment to their psychiatric meds. Every night, the boys lined up by the medication closet and waited their turn for a staff member to hand them a pill along with a tiny paper cup of water. I was told the pills were for anxiety, depression, and more importantly, a guarantee the kids would calm down and sleep through the night. This was a welcome relief for the night staff who looked forward to a quiet shift.

The boys were typical teenagers who wanted to play soccer out in the field or gather around a TV screen and play video games. They were easily distracted and fidgety, which made it a challenge to get them to pay attention while I taught a weekly two-hour lesson that was mapped out in an instructor's manual. The lessons mostly focused on basic life skills and behavior issues like anger management and healthy boundaries. One day, the lesson was on developing empathy.

It was 11 a.m. and time to start the group session. The boys gradually made their way into the classroom to find a seat. Once they were seated, I said, "Okay guys, today's lesson is about empathy. Do any of you know what empathy means?" Silence and blank stares made me grasp for ways to explain the concept of empathy. I clumsily pulled an imagined scenario together. "Let's say you were very close to a younger sister. You notice that lately she rarely comes out of her room. One day you ask her what's up and she starts bawling. She tells you that your uncle had molested her and told her not to tell anyone. She also said she's afraid, confused, and full of shame. How would this make you feel?" No response. Zilch.

The boys continued to fidget in their seats and seemed more interested in watching the clock or looking out the window than participating in the lesson. Based on their clueless expressions, I sensed a possibility that many of them found it difficult or impossible to feel or understand another's pain. This made me wonder, can you teach empathy? An understanding of what it's like to be in someone else's shoes. To have a healthy level of empathy, you should be able to connect with another on a level in which you sense what the other feels. You instinctively want to help end their suffering. Perhaps these boys felt so alone and disconnected from others that they found it impossible to understand or feel another's suffering.

While I didn't see the value in teaching this lesson, I learned about other programs and methods that have proven to be effective in nurturing empathy. The restorative justice approach has been successful by bringing the victim and the offender together for the victim to share their experience and feelings. This approach originated in the 1970s with a probation officer who worked with teens. The purpose is to allow the offender to listen and understand the harm they have caused. This practice not only benefits the victim but the community and the offender as well. It is estimated that communities save $7,000 on each youth who participates because it is more likely he or she will not re-offend.[11]

The greatest, and possibly the most difficult thing I learned during the nine-month internship was not to judge. Period. In the classroom, we learned to "start where the client is" when trying to help someone. To do this, we learned that we must recognize our own personal biases, stereotypes, and prejudices, and then strip them away. We were taught to look at the client as a fellow human who is doing the best they can based on their social and psychological conditioning.

---

11 *Restorative Justice: The Evidence,* Restorative Justice Council, accessed October 24, 2022, https://restorativejustice.org.uk.

While sitting in on therapy sessions with Dr. Moore and the boys, I learned that most of the boys had been horribly abused and neglected themselves while living at home. It wouldn't be long before many of these kids would be sent back to their schools and communities to deal with an avalanche of judgment, disgust, and isolation.

My second internship assignment was at a homeless resource center in downtown Reno. The resource center was a place where the homeless could find information about available services offered around the city. They could put their name on a waiting list to stay in the shelter or find out where and when local charities would be serving food.

While absorbing any information I could about the homeless population, I was most surprised to learn about the growing number of homeless youth living on the streets of Reno. A 2018 report conducted by the Department of Housing and Urban Development (HUD) ranked Nevada #1 in homeless youth.[12] These young adults are generally between 18 and 24 years old. Understandably, they're reluctant to stay in the adult shelter where they risked being preyed upon by the older homeless. They lived and slept in the parks and on the streets of Reno. They were usually overlooked because they didn't stand out like the typical stereotype of a disheveled homeless person pushing a shopping cart. These kids with their backpacks could pass as any typical young person. They wore torn jeans, but they weren't torn on purpose like the latest designer jeans. I've always had a deep sense of compassion for the homeless and at-risk youth. I remembered being a vulnerable pregnant teenager who felt lost many years ago, and that feeling of aloneness was stirred up every time I saw a struggling young person on the street.

---

12 Moser, Molly, and Buergin, Miles, "Nevada ranks highest in unsheltered, homeless youth according to federal report," News 4, December 18th 2018, https://mynews4.com/news/local/nevada-ranks-highest-in-unsheltered-homeless-youth-according-to-federal-report.

FUTURE SOCIAL WORKER

When it was time to graduate, I had mixed feelings. I would miss the camaraderie with my friends as well as the relationships I made with some of the professors, including Mary Hilton who told me not to give up. But I was also chomping at the bit to get out into the world to make a difference.

LEGACY

A week after graduation, on an unusually bleak and drizzly afternoon in May, I found myself in the half-empty parking lot of where I had just taken and passed my social work licensing exam. This was a huge moment for me. Although I didn't have anyone to celebrate with, I could feel Bob's presence. I sat in my car for a long while, and then I began to sob, overcome by a tornado of emotions. I felt relief for passing the exam, uncertainty for the future, and a longing for him, but also a sense of peace knowing that things were going to be okay. Although I couldn't see or touch Bob, I felt his essence surrounding me, and that was the moment I promised him that I would use my degree and the life insurance money to make a difference in the world.

My experience working with homeless youth in San Diego and at the resource center left me with no doubt that I could turn Bob's death into something positive and meaningful. I dreamt about creating a program or service dedicated to helping these young adults. Bob had a rough childhood growing up without a father. His mother had worked two jobs but could barely afford the rent for their one-bedroom apartment. He worked from the age of thirteen to help support his family. It made sense that a project to help these kids would honor his memory. My own story also influenced this developing vision. I felt lost years ago when my mother died and basically lived on my own while skipping school and doing drugs. I also faced the challenge of being pregnant and abused at an early age. I knew what it meant to be "at risk." Along with trusting my intuition about this project, I felt it could extend Bob's life in some way and help to make the world a better place because of him.

> *Intuition is an "inner knowing" or what some call insight or sixth sense. Trusting that gut feeling is an example of when someone follows their spirit. Everyone has intuition but not everyone chooses to listen. Not listening to your intuition is a matter of the ego getting in the way.*

After Bob's death, I passed each day feeling cracked and out of balance. I could now feel myself become grounded and whole again, while I put a plan together that would give support and guidance to these lost kids. My spirit gathered strength as I felt the passion to help these kids rise inside me. An undeniable sense of confidence washed over me as I felt the presence of Bob nudging me to go for it. I felt inspired or "in spirit."

> *Many times, the ego will convince you that you are a victim while leaving you feeling powerless and weak. I remember the temptation to wallow in self-pity after Bob died. It told me, "You're allowed to retreat from life because life has treated you so unfairly." The spirit doesn't accept excuses for your challenges. It understands that life is not supposed to be all butterflies and unicorns. Life is supposed to challenge you. The spirit puts you in charge of managing your life no matter what life hurls your way. My spirit told me, "Shit happens. Dust yourself off and move forward. Look for the rainbow among the clouds. If you can't find one, create one." "Never be a prisoner of your past. Be an architect of your future!"*
>
> – Robin Sharma

INTENTION TO ACTION

To better understand this population of homeless youth, I decided to hold a focus group with the street kids who would regularly gather and hang out during the day on the Downtown Plaza steps next to the Truckee River. On a crisp and pleasant autumn afternoon in 2011, I ordered several pizzas to be delivered to this spot. I introduced myself and told them I wanted to know more about their lifestyles and asked if they would be willing to tell me their stories. One by one, they slowly gathered around me. While they scarfed down the pizza, they shared their stories of abuse, loss, and the realities of life on the streets.

A boy with dark, sunken eyes spoke up, while wolfing down his third slice, and shared how he and his mom had been homeless for the past year, sleeping in unlocked parked cars. He said a week earlier she'd been arrested for prostitution and went to jail, so now he's figuring things out on his own with the help of his new friends.

A quiet boy sitting on a step in the back stood up, went for more pizza, and told of being kicked out of his conservative, religious home after coming out as gay. A goth dressed in all black and wearing a spiked choker disclosed he was attacked and pushed out of the house by his mom's addict boyfriend. He said the rejection hurt most because his mom said nothing as he packed his things, but he understood that she had crack issues of her own.

I instantly connected with one of the girls who was barefoot and obviously pregnant. She looked maybe seventeen or eighteen years old and had a shabby Bohemian style. She wore a tie-dye, wrap-around skirt that fell to her ankles and was held together with a dirty macramé belt. Her hair was down past her waist and decorated with a couple of feathers and some beads. I noticed that her feet were filthy, and I couldn't help but wonder if she could walk on broken glass and put cigarettes out with her soles the way I could when I was her age.

She described how the night before she was offered a place to stay by a friendly-looking older guy who said he had a room in a weekly hotel nearby where she could sleep on the floor. Not wanting to spend another night in the rain, she accepted his invitation and walked a couple of blocks with him to the run-down hotel. She said that once inside, he pulled out a gun and demanded that she go with him to some location and meet a guy who would expect her to do whatever he wanted. She panicked and threw her backpack at him knocking the gun away and ran out onto the streets. I asked her if she called the police, and she gave me a look that said, "Really lady?" Despite my good intentions, I was still naïve.

The street kids were not fans of the local police, who they played cat and mouse with to avoid getting picked up for panhandling, loitering, or illegal camping. If they got caught, they would get a ticket, which they could not pay. They would soon be arrested and sent to the county jail for a night or two. This made no sense to me. How is this helping the city? How is this helping the youth?

While I didn't know exactly what I was going to do for these kids, I knew I would do something. I could use what I learned from school and at my internships to come up with a project that would be effective and meaningful to help these young adults get on their feet.

About a week after meeting with the kids on the plaza, I mentioned to my son, Brian, that I wanted to set up something to help homeless kids, but I wasn't sure what that would look like. He instantly began to come up with ideas. He said, "What about a temporary shelter or a house where they could live long-term?" He went on to say, "Mom, whatever you do, I want in." Brian had been working as a waiter in a restaurant downtown but was feeling unfulfilled. He was twenty-three years old and searching for a way to move forward with his life. From the time he graduated from high school, he had tried being a college student, but it wasn't a good fit. A year had gone by since Bob's death and he was searching for a sense of purpose. The timing of this was perfect.

CHAPTER SEVEN

BRIAN'S STORY

One summer morning about four months after Bob's death, and while I was still in school, I sat at the kitchen table, slowly sipping my coffee as I planned my day. Brian walked in the room, quietly pulled out the chair across from me, and sat down. Tim and Hannah had left the house earlier that morning, so it was just the two of us. We sat in silence. Brian seemed unusually serious as he asked if we could talk. I answered, "Of course," as my stomach tightened, and I prepared myself for whatever was about to drop. I could tell by the intense look on his face that something was very wrong.

Brian and I hadn't seen much of each other lately. He worked nights at a local restaurant and stayed in his room most of the day. He kept his door shut and rarely came out. If I knocked to check how he was doing, he would say, "Fine, I'm just tired." I figured he needed his space after losing his dad and would eventually open up about his feelings, but not until he was ready.

When I was home, my mind was elsewhere. I was trying to figure out how to stay in the house and ahead of the lawsuit. I was going through the checklist of things to do when your spouse dies . . . notify Social Security, the bank, health and car insurance. The list went on. I was also beginning my last year of school. I was trying to maintain control over my life in an unfamiliar world that seemed to have gone insane. Now sitting across the table looking at Brian, I could see that the idea of maintaining total order and control is only an illusion.

> *The ego tells us to fear the unknown. We must maintain control over the people and situations in our life. This is impossible because the only constant in this unpredictable life is change. The spirit tells us to be comfortable with uncertainty. Accept that people and situations don't always match our expectations. Yes, control what you can, but let go of what you can't.*

His eyes teared up as he told me he had been using heroin and needed help. The words seemed to come out of his mouth in slow motion. I told myself to breathe deeply as the reality of this bombshell was sinking in. I thought about the signs I missed. A stream of tears covered his face as he repeated the words, "I'm so sorry, Mom. I'm so sorry, Mom." Suddenly, the pain that engulfed our home rose to a new suffocating level. I hugged him. I reassured him that we would figure this out together and things would work out. I wasn't sure these words were true, but I said them anyway.

Early the next morning, Brian and I were back at the kitchen table. I began making calls to find help. Although I was in the field of social work and thought I knew the system, I was in for a big surprise. I started searching for treatment centers and found there were only two in Reno. Both were full and not taking new patients for at least eight to ten months. I noticed that Brian was starting to sweat, and his face looked pale. His immediate need was to get to a detox clinic as his body was withdrawing from the drug.

After making a few more calls, we connected with the county detox clinic and learned they had one spot that would become available that evening. It was a ten-day supervised stay in a cramped facility next to the homeless shelter. Brian quickly packed what they told him to bring and drove himself to the center. Later, he told me that when he checked himself in and was assigned a cot, he spent his time feeling sick with nausea and chills while a nurse checked his vital signs two or three times a day.

I called Andrea right after Brian left for the clinic. I knew her son, Mike, had a history of alcohol abuse. After seeking treatment and attending AA meetings, he was now in recovery. At Andrea's urging, Mike called to help. The two of us spent the day making calls to several treatment programs around Reno. After continuously being told there was no room for Brian, Mike finally found an opening in a three-month program in Watsonville, a town on the central coast of California.

I spoke with the director of admissions and told him about Brian's situation and that he was currently at a detox clinic. He explained that many addicts believe they don't need additional help after a detox experience and statistically 80 percent fall back into the addiction without the intense counseling and healing that their program offered. He said Brian would most likely need to be convinced to go into treatment and explained that an intervention specialist named Mark would come to the house before Brian was released from the detox clinic. He advised me to arrange for family members to be at the house for support when Brian came home. Mark would facilitate the intervention and hopefully, Brian would agree to the program. Mark would then chaperone Brian back to California.

He gave me a list of things Brian would need for his three months stay and told me to have his bag packed so they could immediately leave for the center after the intervention. Mike and I agreed this was the best, and in reality, the only option that Brian had. Mike also offered to help bring the family together.

THE FIGHT INSIDE

Mike was living in the San Francisco Bay area and took time off from his job as the manager of a large organic foods store. He arrived in Reno two days before Brian was released. Mike was tall, handsome, and wise for his thirty-five years. His upbeat personality and infectious smile drew people in wherever he went. He was glad to help and understood addiction and what Brian was going through. It was comforting to have him there for support. Andrea and her husband Joe immediately flew to Reno from their home in San Jose, Mexico. Michele drove from San Diego and arrived the next day.

Mark arrived at the house the morning before Brian would be released. I introduced myself and the rest of the family before we all sat down to talk. He looked like a middle-aged bodybuilder. I noticed the large dragon tattoos he had on both forearms. He warned us that there was a good chance Brian would get angry after realizing we secretly planned this intervention, and that Brian may feel that we were forcing him into treatment. Mark told us not to worry because he would take care of the situation if it got out of hand; he had years of experience facilitating interventions and everything would be fine. He explained the benefits of the program and touted its success rate. He said our role would be to individually tell Brian why we wanted him to get help. After he answered all of our questions and prepped us on what to expect the next day, he left.

I hardly slept that night anticipating what the next day would bring. I woke to a sunny and bitterly cold morning. Fall had arrived with early temperatures hovering around freezing. I got dressed and made my way to the kitchen to get coffee going before everyone woke. The house was quiet as I stood and looked out the window. I thought, "How did things fall apart so badly, this fast?" I yearned for the past when we were a regular, normal, and happy family. Now we were a family in crisis and spinning out of control. Unable to focus through the tears, I took a deep inhale and exhale and redirected my thoughts to what had to be done in preparation for the day.

BRIAN'S STORY

The ego wants you to cling to the past and worry about the future. The spirit is free to experience "what is." In the present moment, we find an inner peace and clarity to respond to whatever is taking place.

As everyone woke and found their way to the kitchen, I put a bowl of fruit salad and granola on the counter. The room soon filled with the smell of strong coffee and the sounds of clanging dishes and nervous chatter. I glanced back out the window and could see Mark walking up the long driveway. He had said he would park his rental car on the street so he wouldn't tip Brian off that something was going on. He was wearing a heavy jacket and leather gloves. I could see his breath as he hastily reached the front porch. I opened the door, and as he commented on the frigid weather, I led him into the living room where everyone had gathered.

We made small talk while nervously waiting for Brian to arrive. The room became silent when we heard Brian pull up in the driveway. He walked in and suddenly stopped when he saw us. He cautiously walked into the living room with a surprised and confused look on his face. He said, "Hello everyone" in a way that sounded more like a question than a greeting. Mark stood up straight and tall matching Brian's height of six-foot-three. He reached out to shake Brian's hand as he introduced himself. Brian's eyes darted around the room, glancing at each one of us, as he slowly sat down. Mark proceeded to talk about the program and why he was there. He explained to Brian that each of us had something to say and asked him to listen. I was first and told Brian how much I loved him and knew he was hurting inside from his father's death. I added that I was there for him no matter what. Everyone else expressed similar feelings of love and support. Mike was last and said he understood that Brian felt alone. He said he also felt alone when he was struggling with addiction. He could be in a room full of people and feel alone. He assured Brian not to feel that way because the room was filled with people who loved him.

Mark asked Brian, "Well, what do you say? Are you ready to go?" Brian anxiously said, "I can't go for a while. I have to take care of things before I go." Mark replied, "Not to worry. Your mom packed everything you will need. I have two tickets to leave for San Jose at three-thirty." Brian shrugged his shoulders and said, "Okay." An hour later they were gone. A sense of relief and hope washed over me. I thought the worst was over. Now was the time for healing.

A month later, Tim, Hannah, and I drove to Watsonville to visit Brian. I sat in the back seat filled with nervous anticipation. I missed him. Worry lurked in the back of my mind. My ego asked, "Would he be resentful that I sent him away? Would he not be happy to see us?" I was filled with self-doubt and angst.

> *This is an example of the ego playing the "What if?" game that is loaded with fear-based assumptions and beliefs rather than truth. Remember what Seneca said: "We suffer more in imagination than in reality." The spirit notices the disturbing feeling that creeps in with the "What if?" game. It says, "Stop the insanity of worrying about things that most likely will never happen. Stay in the present. If obstacles arise, you will handle them as they arise." Random fact here: 85 percent of the things people worry about never happen.*

We stayed in a hotel the night before our visit and arrived at the center early the next morning. The center was in a secluded area outside of Watsonville, surrounded by thick groves of redwood and sycamore trees. A woman with a welcoming smile greeted us at the main entrance and asked us to wait in the lobby while she let Brian know we were there. A few minutes later, Brian came through the door. I hardly recognized my son. The lines in his face and dark circles around his eyes were gone. His smile matched his bright eyes. He lifted me off my feet with his signature Brian hug. He then hugged Hannah and Tim before he led us to a private area outside where we could sit and talk. He told us how glad he was to see us. He said the first week of the program was the hardest while he continued to have withdrawal symptoms. He expressed that he felt good about the program even though it had a strict schedule. He was required to be up at 5 a.m. each morning and ready to participate in individual and group counseling sessions. He looked forward to the late afternoon break when he was able to workout. He read books during the two hours of free time allowed each day. He had to be in bed with lights out by 8 p.m.

We sat and talked for a couple of hours before a staff member interrupted and told us that visiting hours were about to end. We said goodbye to Brian and got into the car for the seven-hour ride home. The mood was elevated and filled with excitement as we commented on how amazing Brian looked and how content he seemed. I felt relieved and hopeful to finally have my son back even though I knew his full recovery wasn't over yet. This would take time. It was a good day.

Two months later, Brian completed the program. Winter had arrived when he came home and returned to his job at the restaurant. For the first time since Bob's death, I felt the family was going to be okay.

Foreclosure notices from the bank piled up in my mailbox while I looked for a new place to live. I found a condo unit in downtown Reno that was close to school and my internship. I signed the papers and moved in within a couple of weeks. Tim and Hannah moved into a small house they bought in Truckee. Brian didn't have a place to live, so he moved in with me until he could find a place of his own. I welcomed this arrangement because I knew the two-bedroom condo would feel empty while I adjusted to the idea of living alone.

THE FIGHT INSIDE

* * *

Two days before Christmas, I answered a call from Andrea. I could barely understand what she was saying. She was crying while trying to catch her breath, but she managed to blurt out, "Mike is gone. He killed himself." My mind rejected what she was telling me as a bolt of shock coursed through my body and I became nauseous. I couldn't process it. Apparently, Mike had relapsed. How could this be possible? Only four months earlier, at Brian's intervention, Mike had been so upbeat, positive, and helpful. But I remembered Mike sharing how he felt lonely in the middle of a room full of people while acting otherwise. I had thought he was talking about how he felt in the past, but I wondered if that was how he felt when we were all together. I reflected on how content Bob had seemed in the days before his suicide. It struck me how the way someone appears on the outside can be a sharp contrast from what they are really feeling inside. What the fuck?

Brian saw Mike's relapse and death as a sign of his own future. It wasn't long before I started noticing Brian's healthy glow disappear and the lines and dark circles around his eyes reappear.

On an overcast February morning, Brian came out of his room and asked if we could talk. It was the same talk we had had several months earlier. As tears ran down his face, he said he felt empty and hopeless inside. He recognized this dark void as the same emptiness that consumed his dad and Mike. He went on to say that while the treatment center taught him about changing his habits and lifestyle, it hadn't helped him figure out how to completely rid himself of the self-destructive pain he felt. He described this void as a hopeless feeling of "fuck it'" along with the knowledge that he didn't even like himself. While he was telling me this, I could see that what happened to Bob was happening to my son. Brian was losing his spirit. His true self.

Brian wiped the tears from his face, sat up straight, and drew in a deep breath. He reached for his laptop and opened it to a website displaying a Buddhist monastery in Thailand. He described the brief moments of peace he'd felt at the treatment center while reading books about Buddhism and spirituality. He wanted to go where the lessons from these books were practiced and studied. He felt if he went there, he would find peace. I could see that Brian was lost and desperately wanted to reconnect with his true self. Unlike Bob, Brian still had a chance. I wrapped my arms around him while I assured him, we would figure out how to make this trip happen.

Brian spent the next week making arrangements to go to Thailand while he detoxed himself at home. The effects of withdrawal weren't as severe this time because he had been using for only a short time. He wrote a letter to the monastery and was accepted to stay as long as he liked, provided he followed the rules and helped with chores. He bought a one-way ticket to Bangkok and off he went with only his passport and backpack.

He didn't have internet access at the monastery, so it was almost impossible to stay in touch. The few times he was able to send an email, he described his daily routine of rising with the sun, completing his chores, and immersing himself in hours of silent meditation. He ate three simple meals of rice soup each day. His bed was a mat placed on a cement floor with a pillow carved from wood. He said he was finding peace at the monastery and thanked me for making this trip possible.

In the last email he sent before he came home, he said his meditation practice had calmed his mind and he felt at peace. He said he no longer felt separate and alone. He felt connected and part of the world for the first time. His perspective shifted from viewing the world as a hostile place to a place full of possibilities. A sense of gratitude and love filled his heart. He said he was sorry for the pain he caused the family and was thankful for the love and support we gave him. He ended with, "I know now that it is all about love." As I read this, I knew he had found his spirit again.

A couple of months passed before Brian called from the airport in Bangkok to let me know he would be back in Reno soon. Most mothers would have been a nervous wreck if they were in my shoes, but my intuition told me he was fine. He was reclaiming his spirit, and everything would be alright. Two days later, while I was finishing schoolwork at the dining room table, he came through the front door. He looked like a vagabond with his weathered backpack and worn-out clothes. I was overcome with joy to see him as he gave me a warm and all-encompassing hug.

We sat on the couch while he told me the details of his adventure. It felt comforting and reassuring to have him back and to see him glow again. The more he spoke, the more I knew this glow would be permanent. He said he felt a renewed sense of hope for his future and although he wasn't sure what career path he would take; he knew it had to include helping others. The timing was right for Brian to help with this developing project.

CHAPTER EIGHT

THE PATH FORWARD

Along with Brian, Tim and Hannah offered their help, which emboldened my effort and opened an outlet where we could support each other through our grief while honoring Bob with something larger than ourselves. I also brought together a group of friends who had backgrounds in social work, and we started working to create the non-profit that is now called Eddy House. Our mission was to help homeless and at-risk youth develop the life skills necessary for sustainable independence.

I had no idea how to do something like this, but with blind faith, I dove into the process. I knew I would figure it out along the way. I would make mistakes, but I would learn from them. I would use my knowledge, skills, values, and intuition to guide the process, and I had the life insurance money to use for funding. The thought of Bob knowing his life insurance would leave me with financial security haunts me to this day. What I did know was that I would put the money toward something good. Something that would make a difference.

THE FIGHT INSIDE

Many people who were aware of my plans thought I was crazy, including a top administrator from the Reno Social Services Department. I arranged a meeting with her to better understand the services available for homeless youth. I told her I knew there was a rise in youth homelessness and wanted to help these kids. I know she found me to be naïve when she said that I didn't understand what I would be getting into by working with these young adults. She basically said they would eat me alive, and described them as hard, manipulative, and lost causes. I began to take her words personally and suddenly felt overwhelmed and hopeless. My ego told me she was probably right, while my spirit urged me to take a step back and breathe. I could tell she was burnt-out and trying to be real with me, but I knew these kids had potential if only given the chance to be seen for who they really are.

> *Taking things personally is a trap of the ego. It places a higher value on others' opinions than our own. It gives others the power to take away our happiness and leaves us to suffer. The spirit objectively sees the situation and understands the words that come from others represent their world view and not our own. Always catch yourself if you feel defensive. This is the ego telling you that you need to be right. Another sneaky trick to look out for.*
>
> *"Don't let the noise of others' opinions drown out your inner voice. And most important, have the courage to follow your heart and intuition."*
>
> *– Steve Jobs*

After two months of intense research and meetings, I decided to focus on housing the kids who were "aging out" of the foster care system. I learned that many of these eighteen-year-old young adults literally leave the system with their belongings in a trash bag and no place to go. Statistically, these kids end up homeless, and for many, homelessness would become their permanent future. The National Alliance to End Homelessness found that over 400,000 youth are currently in foster care. Approximately 20,000 of those youth age out each year. Within eighteen months of emancipation 40-50 percent become homeless.[13] The reality of these kids' lives hit home as I thought about how easily my sisters and I could have been placed in the system during those years when we had little or no adult supervision. I also couldn't help but wonder about Danny from junior high and where he may have ended up.

I decided to open a group home for aged-out foster boys, where they would feel safe and connected while getting their lives together and planning for their future. I arranged for a realtor to show me a few properties, but the second home we looked at was perfect. It was a two-story house on a quiet street in Northwest Reno, near a bus line. It had four bedrooms that were large enough to each fit two twin beds. The downstairs had an open family room and kitchen area. There was also a spacious backyard with a covered porch, an ideal place for a ping pong table. I closed the deal and covered the walls with a fresh coat of paint before I filled the rooms with modern furniture. I knew these kids had grown up with very little, and what they had was most likely second or third-hand and worn out. I felt their surroundings could influence the way they felt about themselves. I had read somewhere, "If you live in trash, you believe you are trash." I wanted them to come back to a clean, bright, and fresh environment that they could call home.

---

13 O'Neale, Shalita, "Foster Care and Homelessness," Foster Focus, accessed October 28, 2022, https://www.fosterfocusmag.com/articles/foster-care-and-homelessness.

WELCOME HOME

The group of social workers I assembled, became our first board of directors. I hired an administrative assistant to help with our application to obtain a 501c3 nonprofit license. This is the coveted permit every nonprofit is required to have. We crafted together policies and procedures as well as financial statements. Brian gladly quit his job serving tables and took on the role of house manager.

In the fall of 2011, after having everything in place, the team officially welcomed eight boys coming out of the foster care system to live at the house. The kids who came to the Eddy House reminded me of stray dogs who were fearful and untrusting of everyone, behavior that is to be expected based on their past experiences. Many had been abandoned or taken from their homes at an early age due to abuse and neglect. They buried their psychological wounds to avoid pain and then built a protective wall around those wounds. Many end up with trust issues that will haunt them their entire lives unless they strip down the layers and examine the source of the hurt.

The negative ego-based thoughts that continuously played over and over in their heads told them they were not good enough and unworthy of love. One of the boys told me that he felt worthless because he believed his mom had chosen drugs over taking care of him, which made him feel she didn't love or want him. This kid suffered from beliefs that were not the truth. Remember, choosing beliefs over truth is a common trick of the ego.

Unfortunately, many of the stories the kids told of living in foster homes were hard to hear. While there are sincere foster parents who welcome the responsibility for the right reasons, there are many who commit to being foster parents only for the money. They provide the bare minimum of care and essentials to the kids. Close to 30 percent of kids are abused while in foster homes. A study done by Johns Hopkins University found that children in foster care are four times more likely to be sexually abused than kids raised in traditional homes.[14] One boy told me how he had to stay in his room until the family finished dinner, and only then would be allowed to come out and eat what was left over. Another resident told me his foster dad brutally beat his younger brother, who wound up permanently damaged from the attack.

Brian and I tried to make the house feel like a home, which was foreign to most of them. We had family dinners and took them out once a week to the movies or a local event. We accepted a couple of interns from the University of Nevada, Reno's Social Work department to assist at the house twice a week. They helped with basic life skills training that included lessons on how to meal plan, shop for food, cook, do their laundry, budget their money, and maintain good hygiene and health. We hired an assistant to help Brian with the day-to-day functions of the house. Brian and the staff worked with each resident on their personal goals and helped them follow up with appointments and getting to and from school and work.

Creating the right balance of structure and freedom was an ongoing challenge. For many of the boys who had been in the system most of their lives, turning eighteen and being out on their own, presented its own challenges. In some ways, it was tough for them to handle this newfound freedom. We had to create rules that included curfews, guest restrictions, chores, etc. We had weekly family meetings to share and talk about issues the kids may be dealing with. A few months after we opened, I could see that we were successful in creating a stable and supportive home environment and a place where the kids felt good about coming home to. A safe place where they felt "accepted and significant."

---

14 "Sex Abuse and the Foster Care System," Focus for Health, accessed Oct 24, 2022. https://www.focusforhealth.org/sex-abuse-and-the-foster-care-system/.

THE FIGHT INSIDE

We didn't and don't judge them because we understand they have been wounded from their pasts. We accept them. When we take the time to be present with them, we can see how each one of them is special in their own way. Being present and giving sincere attention to someone will give them a sense of "being seen." This focused presence lets them know they "matter." This practice of "acceptance and significance" may sound too simplistic, but it works. It's like giving them sunlight and water and watching them blossom. I believe these two concepts are the core of what everyone ultimately desires. Everyone.

> *The ego wants you to feel separate from others and will try to distract you from being present during an interaction. The spirit feels a sense of connection with others and interacts on a level of soul-to-soul. Rather than allow the ego to occupy our thoughts with our future response, or how to turn the conversation onto ourself, listen with presence. When we are present with someone, they feel seen, and the interaction is more authentic and genuine. Maya Angelou said, "People will forget what you said, people will forget what you did, but people will never forget how you made them feel."*

Word was getting out into the community that we were open, and calls began to come in from churches and schools asking if we had room for a young person they knew who needed a home. The principal of the nearby high school called one day and said he had a student showing up for class each day who was homeless. He was seen sleeping in the bushes and cleaning up in the river before school. He asked if we had room. Unfortunately, we were full.

THE PATH FORWARD

SISTER POWER

The first year tested my spirit. I was at Eddy House or in meetings with social services and city officials most of the day and returned home to my condo to work on paperwork until late into the night. Putting together policies and procedures, applying for grants, and filling out forms takes time. This resulted in an average twelve-hour workday, seven days a week. No matter how hard I worked, I always felt as though I was behind and trying to catch up. There were lonely nights in the condo when I was overwhelmed with self-doubt, and I would ask myself if all of this was worth it, or was this project just a way to distract myself from facing the grief of losing Bob? My ego was untethered and running wild.

I would usually call Michele during those times. She would say, "Sis, follow your heart. What is your heart telling you?" Her advice gave me clarity and brought me back into my spirit. I knew in my heart and gut, that I was doing exactly what I should be doing at that particular time. I knew I had gotten off track and would examine my previous thoughts of, "What the fuck am I doing? I'm in way over my head. I'm not strong or smart enough. I'm also throwing my money away and will be totally broke." I would recognize that all these unnecessary fear-based thoughts were coming from my ego and not true. I redirected my thoughts to what was true and coming from my spirit. My previous inner conversation filled with insecurity and self-doubt would change to "I must try and make Eddy House happen because I feel in my core it is the right thing to do. I have the knowledge and I'm capable. What I don't know, I will figure out myself or seek outside advice. I will know when it is rationally time to stop putting my money into Eddy House. I will stick to my budget and no, I won't have to eat dog food when I retire." I found the more I paid attention to my thoughts and saw them for what they were, the easier it became to detect a disturbance early on and take immediate action rather than go down a rabbit hole of insecurity and negativity. Once I was released from the grip of my ego, I felt fueled with a stubborn determination to see that these kids had a chance at life.

> *While writing this book, I have encountered many visits from my ego. It shows up and says, "Who do you think you are, attempting to write a book? You're not a writer. You don't understand sentence structure or even what a preposition is. Why waste your time?" When I have these thoughts, I can feel my body contract, and a sense of self-doubt and insecurity creeps in. Then I follow Michele's advice and do a heart and gut check. My spirit tells me, "Do not be afraid of failure. If I can help ONE reader recognize how to use the power they hold within their own spirit to live a more full and intentional life, then it would be worth it."*

I felt a deep connection with these kids, because I knew what it felt like to be lost and searching for direction at that age. My experience of being seventeen and pregnant was similar to what these kids were going through. The feeling of being alone and afraid. I didn't want these kids to feel alone any longer. I wanted them to feel supported and connected.

Johnny, a quiet kid who had been at the house for a few months, teared up when he asked me to fill out a form from school that asked for information about who the school should notify in case of an emergency. He said he never had a real family before, and in the past, he would have his group home administrator or social worker provide the information. He said his stay at Eddy House was different because he now believed he had a family. Like my intention to write this book, I knew from the start of this project that if I could help *one* kid feel supported and loved, it would all be worth it. This boy made me feel "mission accomplished."

I was fortunate to have Michele to set me straight when I let down my guard and allowed my ego to creep in, but I was also fortunate to have Andrea to rely on when it came to making critical and rational decisions. As I saw my bank account continue to shrink, I would call Andrea for her advice. These calls would come when I had to realistically ask myself, at what point would I have to call it quits? She knew how much this project meant to me, but she also knew that my personal expenses were low, so she would say, "You should be fine for now, but you will have to find other ways to support the house and staff."

FOLLOW THE MONEY

Trusting Andrea's advice, I knew that for this to work, I would need financial support from the community. I didn't enjoy networking but knew that I had to get myself out there and talk about the project. I tried to set up meetings with people who were involved in the community and had a lot of influence. Many of these people were from well-established families in Reno that were usually connected to the casinos back in the day. Unfortunately, I was new to Reno and didn't know any of these people. I was able to get contact referrals from my friends in social work, but I found it almost impossible to get through. I left messages that introduced myself followed by a request to return my call. After failing to get a single response, a friend advised me to switch my California phone number and area code to a Nevada number. Apparently, many established Nevadans didn't like the influx of people moving into Reno from California. I did and it worked.

I soon began to have success at setting up meetings. I called these meetings my "put on the red dress," meetings. I was turned down many times because they felt I was giving these kids a handout and not a hand up. They believed everyone should suck it up and pull themselves up by their bootstraps, no matter what their circumstances were. Of course, these were the views of people who always had support from their inner circle of privilege. On one occasion, when I was about to be turned away from a potential donor because he had this belief, I asked him if he had children. He said he had a teenaged son and daughter. I asked him if he felt they would be successful if sent out into the world at the age of eighteen without any family support or a safety net. I asked him to remember when he was eighteen and how that would have felt for him. I left that meeting with a small check and a sense that I opened his heart.

I seemed to have success getting through to potential donors with statistics and facts about the social and economic costs of homeless youth to the community. I explained that HUD estimated the annual cost of a homeless person to the community was $36,000.[15] These costs come from shelters, emergency rooms, jails, detox centers, etc. I also told them that if we don't help a homeless youth, while at this vulnerable age, they will most likely face a lifetime of homelessness—and the associated costs to the city that go with it.

I learned that, if I couldn't convince some people through their heart, I had a chance if I approached them through their wallet. But many times, there was no convincing them, no matter what I said. I found myself becoming frustrated because it was harder than I expected to raise money from these wealthy individuals. Although they had more than enough material wealth, which was obvious by the mansions they lived in—or the many cars they kept in their garages—they were resistant to give away any part of it, even if it could help others in need.

---

15 "What is the Cost of Homelessness?" Father Joe's Villages, March 8, 2022, https://my.neighbor.org/what-is-the-cost-of-homelessness/.

The ego tries to distract you from your true self by encouraging you to falsely identify your self-worth by the value of your possessions. This mindset can lead to greed and a sense of never having enough. The spirit knows you are more than your role, status, or possessions. If these were taken away from you . . . you would be ok. The spirit finds joy in sharing and sees the abundance in life.

Okay, I must check my own ego here. It sounds like I'm making judgments and assumptions. It's possible these wealthy people may give generously to another cause or maybe my pitch needed work. Hey, I never said I was perfect.

While looking for additional funding strategies, I read about the Delancey Street Project in San Francisco, which housed ex-prisoners with the hope of reintegrating them back into society.[16] It was founded in 1971 by an ex-addict, John Maher, who created a family-like rehabilitation center. Today, it operates various businesses such as restaurants, catering, and moving companies that are completely managed and run by the residents. The businesses serve as a funding source as well as an opportunity to employ the residents and provide them with job skills and work experience. I loved this model and wanted to replicate it at Eddy House. I had many ideas for a business, ranging from a recycling center to a pet grooming business, but nothing felt right.

A year had passed since the house opened. A typical day revolved around driving the kids to and from appointments, school, or work. Brian, the staff, and I helped with homework, job applications, resumes, and tasks like opening a bank account or getting a driver's license. The kids took turns planning and preparing dinner each night. Spaghetti or tacos were the common choice.

---

16 https://www.delanceystreetfoundation.org

While the house was up and running, I continued to search for a business idea. One afternoon in September, I happened to be visiting Tim and Hannah at their home in Truckee. Hannah was excited to tell me she had just come from a food and craft fair in town where she met someone selling pot pies. She raved about how delicious they were and told me she met the owner. He ran a successful restaurant in Placerville, California, called Z Pie and wanted to start opening more restaurants. I looked up his website and read about franchise opportunities. It explained that a potential franchise owner would have Z Pie's full support with opening and operating a Z Pie restaurant. This sounded like a good fit with Eddy House.

The next day I went to the fair to meet Kevin Coots, the owner, and learn more about the business. We talked about how his operation worked and what it would entail to open a franchise in Reno. Two days later, we met at a coffee shop in Reno and signed a contract to open a restaurant. We immediately secured permits and licenses and went to work renovating an old building located downtown that had previously been a market. I hired a couple of experienced managers but otherwise, all positions were filled by the boys from Eddy House.

Four months later, the restaurant was ready to open. The kids were enthusiastic, and after being trained, they were eager to start working. For many, it was their very first job. The opening was successful and attracted media coverage that included interviews with some of the boys and a general overview of what we were about. This brought in business as well as donations.

WIDOW'S CLUB

A few days after Z Pie opened, I received a letter in the mail. It was from a man who'd seen my story in the local paper. He said he got emotional when he read about Eddy House and wanted to help. The letter included a check for $3,000. I suddenly felt backed by the community. More letters followed that included checks and promises to visit the restaurant. Some also included personal stories of having been through the foster system or losing a family member to suicide.

I also received a few letters from widows who read about my story and wanted to know how I'd kept myself going after losing Bob. One morning, while going through my mail, I opened a letter from a woman named Susan, whose husband had died a month earlier from a heart attack. She described the deep hole she felt in her heart, the hole I was familiar with. Susan said she felt lost and didn't know how to move forward without him. I imagined the tears she must have shed as she wrote this letter. I also understood that she felt a desperate need to heal and was searching for a path out of her darkness.

I began to receive more letters like this one. They were so personal that I felt a written response would be inadequate, so I offered to meet up, usually in a coffee shop, to talk about our common experience with grief. I instantly felt a strong bond with these women, who all understood how life can kick your ass when you suddenly lose your partner and best friend. It felt good to find this widow tribe who was going through things that your girlfriends or even family members couldn't understand. Things like suddenly sleeping alone, eating alone, basically doing everything "alone." No longer having that person around to share how your day was going or take care of you when you got sick. Also, learning new skills like how to take care of your car or household repairs. This was all new to me after thirty-four years of having Bob to rely on. Looking back, I would call this "learned helplessness." We talked about how a song or a smell could suddenly trigger an emotional meltdown, without warning, at any given time or place. I compared this to a thunderstorm and could feel that as time moved on, the storms would pass over with less frequency and intensity.

As I met and talked with these women, I felt they were expecting me to have all the answers on how to successfully move forward after losing your partner. They all felt stuck and were looking for any sign or glimpse of hope, that it could be possible to find life meaningful again in these lonely uncharted waters. I certainly didn't have all the answers, but I knew that going deep into my spirit gave me strength. That solid part of me that couldn't be threatened or harmed by anything the world threw at me. Not even losing Bob. Creating this project was fueling my spirit as I moved on with my life.

> *The ego wants you to fully identify and attach to an **illusion** of who you truly are. The ego told me, "You are defined as 'Bob's wife' and without that role any longer, I would be nothing. My spirit knew that when you are stripped from your attachments you realize the truth of who you really are. My spirit said, "I am no longer Bob's wife. Now is a time to reimagine myself and my place in the world. Relationships and experiences always change, but my true self remains constant."*

SOLO

Two years had passed since Bob's death, and with the urging of a few girlfriends, I jumped into the online dating pool. After making a connection on Match.com, I found myself sitting outside on the patio of the local Starbucks waiting to meet this person. I looked up when I heard a voice say, "Are you Lynette? I'm John." An athletic-looking man with a boyish glint in his eyes smiled as he pulled out a chair and sat across from me. After that introduction, things clicked.

We began to spend more time together going out to dinner, concerts, events, or just relaxing at each other's homes. A few months into our relationship, I felt myself trying to please him while pretending to enjoy things that I hated. I watched Nascar on TV. I prepared his favorite meals although I didn't like them. I was trying to be someone he would want, but it was not me. It soon became apparent we were two different souls with opposite perspectives on how we viewed the world and each other. I found myself blaming him for making me feel like a miserable victim when, in fact, it was my fault for trying to force a square peg into a round hole. I could no longer escape the truth of why I stayed: I was afraid to be alone.

At this point, I did what I always do when I feel as though I'm losing myself. I wrote in my journal to help sort things out. I took long contemplative hikes. I relied on my spirit to guide me in the right and true direction. While the voice from my ego told me I couldn't be happy alone, the voice from my spirit began to emerge as if coming out of a deep coma and told me that was bullshit. She said, "Seriously, girl, what the hell are you doing? Stop with this helplessness crap and leave. You've got this!" I listened to that voice and left the relationship.

> *The ego wants you to feel incomplete and not enough without a partner. The spirit knows you are complete just the way you are. The belief that another will fill your void and make you happy is a trick of the ego. The spirit knows you can't expect someone to "fix" you. A successful relationship involves partners who are good with themselves and strong in their spirits.*

It wasn't long before loneliness was replaced with the joy of living life on my own terms while embracing all the freedom and independence that came with it. If I wanted to have popcorn and champagne for dinner and watch a Netflix series alone, I did and I loved it. Rather than looking for someone to make me feel happy and complete, I became that someone.

SWAN SONG

I once read that the Dalai Lama doesn't engage in romantic relationships because the emotions, both positive and negative, take away from our peace and inner joy. He says that romantic relationships can create an emotional rollercoaster. You spend emotional energy to solidify the relationship and then again to hold on to it. He adds that it is better to not be distracted by romantic desires, which involve a conditional give and take of personal power. He believes true peace and happiness are achieved through a life free of drama and with consistent love for all. He has a point, but what about the natural forces of sexual energy that come with human connection? After John and I broke up, and having no interest in dating again, I was beginning to accept that being solo could result in losing that part of the human experience for the rest of my life—until a night out with Karin.

A year after my relationship with John ended, I entered the dimly lit bar inside the Grand Sierra Hotel and Casino looking to meet with my friend Karin. Karin and I instantly became good friends from the time we met at a social event several months earlier. I admired her adventurous and curious spirit, which had taken her traveling around the world solo. She never married and says yes to life. I spotted Karin waving and pointing to an empty seat next to her, which I immediately claimed. Moments later, I felt a tap on my shoulder and glanced over to see two fine-looking men, who were at least ten years our junior, standing behind us. The one who looked like a younger and taller George Clooney leaned close into me and with a slight southern drawl said, "Excuse me, but would you ladies mind if we join you?" That's how the evening started.

Our newfound friends were pilots who had just flown into town from Nashville and were planning to head back to the east coast the next day. As the bartender kept replenishing our drinks, we organically separated into pairs. "George Clooney," a.k.a. Scott, and I engaged in our own conversation while Karin and the other handsome pilot went into their own bubble.

Our talking turned into kissing, and then he asked me if I wanted to go up to his room. Without hesitation, I nodded to Karin who smiled back with a thumbs up, and Scott and I headed toward the elevator. Off I went with Scott to his room. The night was a whirlwind of passion with a few water breaks. In the morning, I did the walk of no shame to my car, beaming with a celestial glow and holding my head high. I couldn't wait to get home and call Michele. She listened to my story and then said, "Lynette, you are now an official senior slut. You go, sister!" I called Karin and learned she had also done the walk of no shame that morning right before me.

The experience of that night left me with a new perspective on dating and seeking romantic relationships. Although Scott was exceptional in every way, and the chemistry between us was over the top, I didn't have that past desire to attach and cling. I didn't need to ask the question, "When can I see you again?" or carry the anxiety of wondering if he liked me. I took it for what it was. The enjoyment of two people being present with each other without expectations, commitments, compromises, or sacrifices.

SINGLISM

After working a long day at the restaurant, I went to dinner at the home of two close friends, Carol and Ben. I first met Carol when I volunteered with the Red Cross in San Diego during the Southern California fires of 2008. We were both assigned to the hot shot crew and became instant friends. Carol and Ben have been married for more than twenty years.

After dinner, while the three of us were enjoying the end of a good bottle of wine, Ben said, "Gee Lynette, I feel bad you're alone and wish you would find someone." I noticed Ben had the same look on his face that Lauren (a friend's daughter) had years ago when she affectionately said, "I'm so sorry you won't go to heaven with me because you're not Mormon." I remember thinking she must have envisioned me burning up in hell for eternity, and now Ben pictures me home alone surrounded by cats. Rather than attempt to convince him that I enjoyed my solo life, I said, "Ben, I know you're coming from a caring place but no need to worry for me. I'm good."

Both Ben and Lauren spoke with sincerity and compassion, but it was the pity in their voices that made me uncomfortable. I knew Ben viewed me as incomplete or lacking without a partner in my life. A few days after that dinner, I got a text message from another friend, Alicia. She texted, "Hey I heard about this single guy I want to fix you up with. Tell me your schedule." I responded, "Thanks for the thought but I'll pass. You know I'm not interested in dating. I'll let you know if I change my mind." Although I sounded like I left the door open, I knew I wouldn't change my mind because after experiencing both single life and coupled life, I much preferred my solo status.

On a Friday night, I met Raine at our local hangout, Shenanigans, for happy hour. Raine is one of my single 3 a.m. girlfriends and my "go-to" if I have something on my mind. She sees things from all angles and with clarity. I saw Raine heading toward the entrance just when I pulled up in front. Her thick brown hair was loosely pulled up in a scrunchie. She wore her trademark cowgirl boots that complemented her downhome but sophisticated style. She waited while I parked and then we went inside together.

When we found a table, I ordered my usual Sam Adams draft and french fries. Raine ordered the same. The cold mugs of beer arrived, we clinked our glasses, and after a dramatic exhale I unloaded, "Okay, sister, I have to vent. So, I was invited to Sandy's daughter's wedding, and the invitation said to RSVP with the name of your plus one. Hell, I left it blank thinking if I don't have a plus one, does that mean I'm a minus one? Then at the wedding, the tables were all set for six. I sat with Susie and Ron and Jane and Steve, so that was fun, but it was awkward to sit next to an empty chair and place setting. I guess they figured I forgot to add my plus one. Well, then the first thing Susie says is, 'So who are you dating?' Seriously, after not seeing her for over a year, my love life was all she cared about? Then, by the end of the dinner, Jane is trying to fix me up with a friend of a friend who just got divorced. Why is it so hard for people to accept that I just might like my single life?"

Raine smacks the foam off her lips after a healthy gulp of beer and says, "Yeah, it's annoying how singles are dissed. I found out I pay the same fee at my gym that a married couple does. And what about the tax breaks, insurance, and social security benefits couples get that singles don't? It's not right."

The noise level rose as more of the Friday night crowd showed up. Suddenly, I noticed Jim and Marsha coming through the door. Jim had on his usual scowl face, which said, "I don't want to be here. My wife dragged me out." Marsha, a petite blonde who is at least ten years younger than Jim, followed him to a table in the corner. I said to Raine, "Why is Marsha with Jim? He's a miserable jerk, and she is so sweet." (Okay, I know that statement was full of judgment and didn't come from my higher self. Again, I'm not perfect.)

Raine's response was direct and short, "She's afraid to be alone." The rest of the evening was filled with more rounds of beer, lots of laughter, and conversations with other Shenanigan regulars. As I'm getting ready to leave and putting on my coat, I notice Marsha and Jim still sitting in the dark corner. They are both looking off in different directions, and I'm wondering if they even spoke to each other the entire evening. I thought, "How can two people be together and look so alone?" And then I remembered the heavy silence and moments of forced conversation that best describe the date nights Bob and I had in the final years.

It was hard to fall asleep that night as I recalled the last year of being Bob's wife. While we were only an inch away from each other in bed, it felt like we were miles apart. The loneliness I felt was compounded by the burden of pretending we still shared a strong bond. We were once soul mates and then became strangers. I wondered what his secrets were but was too afraid to ask. He kept his distance fearing I would ask.

Along with Ben and Alicia, many others in our society believe that a single status is a signal you must be damaged goods with either questionable baggage or have a commitment phobia. It's believed a single person could never be happy while living alone. Many people think singles sit around moping about their single status. In fact, studies have shown the happiest and healthiest demographic is single women with social connections.[17] They found that single women are more apt to build strong relationships because they have the space in their lives for quality time with friends and family. Rather than focusing on one person, they have multiple deep and fulfilling relationships. They also enjoy the freedom to be in charge of how they manage their finances, and how they spend their time. Another common myth about single people is they will die alone. Logic says one person in a couple will die first, which leaves the other in the same boat; however, studies have shown singles have a larger social network of support than their married friends, and actually live longer.

In a scene from *Sex and the City*, Carrie said, "The most exciting, challenging, and significant relationship of all is the one you have

---

[17] Patrick, Wendy L., "Why Many Single Women Without Children Are So Happy," Psychology Today, February 28, 2021, https://www.psychologytoday.com/us/blog/why-bad-looks-good/202102/why-many-single-women-without-children-are-so-happy.

with yourself. And if you find someone to love the you that you love, well that's just fabulous." I would add that if that happened it would be added sprinkles to an already decorated cupcake.

BRIGHTER CANDLE

With both Eddy House and Z Pie up and running, it was inspiring to see the kids interact with the customers and feel part of the community rather than unwelcome outcasts. It was obvious to see their self-esteem grow as they stood taller and made direct eye contact with the customers. This new sense of confidence was bolstered as they earned a paycheck and opened their first bank accounts. The staff at the house helped them manage their money, and soon a couple of the boys bought their first cars.

A year and a half after opening Eddy House, I continued to feel like a one-man army and rarely took time out to reflect on what the project meant to the community or how it had evolved into something meaningful. I was surprised when the dean of the school of social work at the university called to ask if I would be available to be the keynote speaker at the upcoming graduation ceremony. Of course, I said yes, but I thought to myself, "How am I ever going to find the time to write a speech and practice it?" I figured I would find time because graduation was a full month away. I finally sat down and wrote my speech the day before graduation.

Then, it sank in. It had only been two years since I graduated and four years since I sat in that restroom stall and cried because I felt I wouldn't be able to keep up. I remembered how I had fallen for the ego traps of comparison and not feeling good enough. Since then, my spirit has only grown stronger. Yes, I gave the speech, and delivered it with confidence and enthusiasm.

CHAPTER NINE

NEW DIRECTIONS

As time passed, I noticed larger numbers of homeless kids wandering the streets or congregating by the river and bus station. I recalled the grim facts I learned during my internship. Nevada is ranked highest in the nation for youth homelessness, with 1,400 homeless kids living on the streets. Realizing this is a growing crisis, I felt it was time for Eddy House to step up and help more of these forgotten and neglected kids. Yes, we were helping seven or eight boys at a time at Eddy House, but what about the hundreds of young adults left out on the streets?

I was also facing the fact that after two years of doing my best, Z Pie was not turning a profit. I hired a marketing firm to help with branding and a publicity campaign. I tried to branch out by catering to local businesses. I added new items to the menu and set up an outside dining area in the adjacent courtyard. Despite all these efforts, the restaurant continued to lose money, and my bank account continued to shrink. Andrea was sounding increasingly nervous and more serious with her advice. Besides losing money on the restaurant, I was spending most of my time and energy on the business aspects of the project, which I didn't enjoy. Profit and loss statements and food cost analysis did not stoke me out.

I learned to pay attention to my intuition, and it told me we should change course to help the vast numbers of homeless youth who were left behind. I researched how other communities dealt with their homeless youth population and realized the city lacked a drop-in center, a place for kids to come and feel safe while getting their basic needs met. It only made sense these kids wouldn't be ready to look for a job or go back to school. They are always in survival mode, looking for food or a shower, never mind a place to sleep. A drop-in center had to happen.

I put together a business plan for an Eddy House drop-in center and talked about it at meetings that were led by the community foundation. Fortunately, we were able to get the financial support of a few major donors and other community stakeholders and decided to close the restaurant and focus on opening a drop-in center.

We found a convenient downtown location close to the river and bus station where the kids hung out. The drop-in center would occupy an old Victorian house. It had several rooms that included two showers, a kitchen, and space for cots and group sessions. We scheduled qualified professionals to come in and offer resources to the kids such as counseling, health care, employment, and educational assistance.

WHAT'S IT LIKE?

A week before the Eddy House drop-in center opened, a small group of community supporters and I spent three days and two nights sleeping on the streets and eating at the soup kitchen with the kids.

We wanted to experience what these youth went through each day and night, and to better understand the physical and emotional challenges they faced. We coordinated the timing of our third and last day on the street with the opening. We hoped our effort would draw enough media attention to help gain public support. Our group of six included Brian, Pat Cashell, who was the manager of the city's homeless shelter, and three other community activists.

We met downtown on a chilly March morning with our backpacks and sleeping bags. We aimlessly walked the streets and introduced ourselves to any lost-looking kid we encountered. We learned many of them slept in groups of three so that one could stay awake and keep watch for potential attacks or prevent being robbed. It was heartbreaking to hear their stories of being hungry, afraid, cold, and tired every night while they searched for a place to sleep. One girl told me she regularly snuck into a casino and locked herself in a restroom stall where she spent the night to stay warm. This worked if she got past security, which was difficult, because they're trained to watch out for kids with backpacks and kick them off the premises. She occasionally rode the bus all night, which was another way to find warmth and safety. They also told us stories of selling their bodies to get food or of being robbed.

We learned that many of the youth would hang out in the bus station until it closed. We joined them as darkness set in and the temperature dropped. When the bus station closed, we were asked to leave and reluctantly walked toward the river to find a place to sleep. I remember how scary and harsh the street felt. It was the same street I walked down many times during the day feeling carefree and safe. The alleys I passed in the daytime had transformed into pop-up drug dens and street brothels. The sounds and shadows bouncing off their walls felt threatening. My heart raced, and I could feel my chest tighten as I held on to the sides of my backpack and tried not to make eye contact with the strangers who passed by. The night felt bitterly cold and lonely. We wandered off the street and away from the dimly lit streetlights to find a place to sleep. We climbed down a steep embankment by the river and crawled into our sleeping bags. The next morning, we heard that a stabbing and a rape took place not far from our camp. Just another night on the streets.

THE EDDY HOUSE DROP-IN CENTER IS OPEN!

After our final night, we were scheduled to be at the Eddy House drop-in center by noon for the opening. As we walked closer to the center, we were greeted by anxious reporters who wanted to know about our experience on the streets and what Eddy House was all about. I told them I witnessed a side of Reno that resembled a third-world country. People in our own community were hungry, terrified, and just trying to stay alive while navigating the challenges of living on the streets.

I also told them many of the homeless I met were young. I explained how the Eddy House drop-in center would provide basic needs and support services to these desperate kids. While talking to reporters, nagging thoughts surfaced in the back of my mind. Will any of these kids come? Was I wrong in my estimation of the need? Will the new staff and the board of directors be disappointed and lose faith in me?

> *Fear of failure is another tactic of the ego. Remember the ego wants you to go through life playing it safe and staying in your comfort zone. This leads to stagnation, complacency, and an unfulfilled life. The spirit wants you to reach your full potential and live the best version of yourself. It says, "So what if you fall down a few times? Success only comes from trying things out. Just think of what you would do if you knew you wouldn't fail."*
>
> *"Destroy your fears so you can take risks. Destroy your ego so you can see life."*
>
> *– Maxime Lagace.*

NEW DIRECTIONS

My fears disappeared after the press and city officials left and several scruffy-looking kids began to show up. Soon, the house was bustling while the staff guided them to a bathroom where they could take a shower or to the large kitchen where most filled their pockets with snacks for later. Watching them as they scarfed down hot food dropped off by a local church group convinced me that what I'd felt in my heart and gut had been right. The Eddy House drop-in center would be a safe place for eighteen to twenty-four-year-old young adults to escape the nightmare of surviving on the street. And it was needed.

The early days were a little overwhelming. The staff was stretched thin while trying to keep both the center and the house running smoothly. More and more kids showed up at the center each day. Although the house had been a success over the past three years, it was becoming a drain on resources better used at the drop-in center. It became evident that we would be more effective to follow our mission if we closed the house and solely focused on the center. The timing was right to close the house. Many of the residents were ready to transition into their own places and move on with their lives. When the house was emptied and put on the market, I reflected on what had already been accomplished and felt energized about what was to come.

It wasn't long before the youth felt ownership of the drop-in center, and along with the staff, created a sense of family and a safe place to shake off the stress from the street. The kids pitched in to help keep the place clean and organized. They also kept each other in check to prevent arguments from brewing or drama to escalate. The drop-in center was most likely the only place where they felt welcomed and accepted. Many of the kids who came had been abused, neglected, and rejected for most of their young lives and this safe place gave them temporary relief from all the ugliness on the streets but more importantly, a sense of hope.

Our programming is based on the trauma-informed care model, which recognizes the true effect trauma has on someone. Instead of asking a kid, "What's wrong with you?" we ask, "What happened to you?" The staff worked with the kids on all aspects of their lives, but mainly the trauma they had buried deep in their psyches. It is ultimately about examining their psychological wounds and putting them on a path to heal their broken spirits.

TIME TO LEVEL UP

Although the Eddy House drop-in center was fulfilling the needs of the youth, it was only open from 10 a.m. to 5 p.m. during the week and closed on weekends. The safety and resources we provided during the day ended when we had to close our doors and they had to return to the streets. The board of directors and I were determined to find funding and open a new location that could facilitate a 24/7 center.

Eddy House recently celebrated its ten-year anniversary and currently has a strong and cohesive board of directors along with a dedicated and focused executive director, who has taken Eddy House to the next level. Eddy House now has a main 24/7 drop-in shelter and a full range of supportive services for the youth. The facility offers job training and educational resources as well as clinical counseling and a wide variety of social services on site. In addition, Eddy House operates two transitional homes for the youth who are ready to be on their own.

IT TAKES A VILLAGE

One of the most rewarding aspects of creating Eddy House is to see the community step up and support the kids. At the start of this journey, I felt confused and frustrated when I was repeatedly turned down after asking for funding. I thought no one cared. I realized later that rather than being a community of cold-hearted and uncaring people, our community consisted of great people who simply weren't aware of the situation. This gives truth to the concept that the first step to change is awareness. Oh, and don't assume!

Over time, it has been exalting to see the community rally their support for the youth. Acts of kindness and compassion regularly show up at the doorstep when someone reaches out to donate or volunteer. The kids hold their heads a little higher with a growing sense of community and belonging to something larger than themselves. Life no longer feels hostile and against them. It now feels inclusive and full of possibilities.

We have witnessed many kids progress to a point where they are independent and contributing back to the community, rather than forever living a life of homelessness and being a burden. I truly believe that putting our resources into prevention and helping the homeless youth can pretty much end the cycle of homelessness. We have the data and outcomes that prove this is not only possible, but we are doing it, and it works!

Recently, representatives from the U.S. Department of Housing and Urban Development flew to Reno from Washington D.C. to tour Eddy House. They were so impressed by what they saw and learned that they officially recognized Eddy House as a national model.[18] They understand that every city in the U.S. would benefit from having an Eddy House in their community. Dream on!

---

18 Marks, Eric, "Eddy House earns EnVision Center designation," This Is Reno, October 23, 2020, https://thisisreno.com/2020/10/eddy-house-earns-envision-center-designation-photos/

CHAPTER TEN

EVERYONE NEEDS A HOME

About fifteen years ago, I read an article in the *New York Times* about a homeless man who had died on a busy sidewalk in Manhattan during the winter while trying to sleep over a subway grate to keep warm. No one knew for sure how long he had been dead while hundreds of people walked around him daily, but the coroner figured he had been on the sidewalk for a few weeks after he froze to death. I remember feeling a mix of sadness and anger when I read this story, thinking a dog would never be allowed to freeze to death on a busy sidewalk. Someone would surely step up and do something. I wondered how humans could be so fearful and detached from one another.

> *The ego wants us to feel separate from others. It wants to keep us in a fearful state while conjuring countless ways others could harm us. Ironically, the root of this fear is our fear of rejection or abandonment. As humans, we all want to be accepted and loved*

but the ego tells us not to trust one another. Others are a threat and not like us. The spirit tells us we are all the same and embraces the concepts of oneness and love. When you help another, you help yourself. We are all connected.

I realized this act of detachment was happening not only in big cities like New York but also in my own community. When I was an intern at the homeless resource center in 2011, I stood by and watched EMTs maneuver the frozen body of a homeless person into a body bag. I learned this happens several times a year when the shelter runs out of space or when someone gets high enough to pass out on the sidewalk. In 2021, the Reno coroner's office recorded that fifty-four homeless individuals died alone and outside that year.[19] These occurrences rarely make the news because unfortunately, no one seems to care.

ROBERT

When I began my internship at the homeless resource center, I didn't know much about the homeless, other than they must have issues with addiction or mental illness to live a life on the streets. I later learned that many are homeless simply because they ran into tough times and couldn't afford rent. Although people are homeless for different reasons, the one thing they have in common is that no one wants them around.

The only homeless person I knew before my internship was a disheveled, red-faced, older man named Robert. He babbled to

---

19 Robinson, Mark, "A look at Washoe County's 54 homeless deaths last year; vigil set for Wednesday," Reno Gazette Journal, February 22, 2022, https://www.rgj.com/story/news/2022/02/22/vigil-homeless-people-died-washoe-county-2021-reno-city-plaza/6883124001/.

himself while he sat on the same bench every day two blocks from my condo. I passed him almost daily when I took Otis out, and he always smiled when he saw us coming. He was particularly happy to see Otis, whom he called "Champ." Otis, being a lab, always had a tennis ball in his mouth and would push it into Robert's hand, hoping Robert would go for the bait and throw it, which Robert gladly did.

Robert and I soon became trusted friends. He would call me "Sweet Girly," and I would listen to him ramble about Martians coming to get him or tales of encounters with the Secret Service. It was obvious Robert suffered from delusional voices in his head and what would be labeled a serious mental illness. Seeing the fear in Robert's eyes and hearing the paranoia in his voice, I wondered if Robert's condition and other serious mental illnesses could be interpreted as an out-of-control ego, like a runaway train overloaded with fear-based thoughts.

I thought of all the disorders I read about in the DSM (*Diagnostic and Statistical Manual of Mental Disorders*). The most common criteria used to label many of these illnesses and disorders, all featured egoic fear-based characteristics. While looking over this list, I realized we all have been consumed by some of these afflictions from time to time, and consequently, we suffered. I found it interesting that no spirit-based criteria were found in its 940 pages. Here is a sample:

- Suspicious of others
- Feelings of sadness, guilt, shame, hopelessness, helplessness, and low self-esteem
- Lack of self-confidence and judgment or abilities
- Social isolation
- Fear of criticism or rejection
- View of self as inferior to others
- Worry-anticipating the worst
- Self-concept centers around beliefs of inadequacy, worthlessness, and low self-esteem

THE FIGHT INSIDE

- Fear of losing control
- Envy or resentment toward those more fortunate
- Pessimistic
- Judgmental toward others
- Fear of loss of support or approval
- Unstable self-image or sense of self
- Chronic feelings of emptiness

While Robert's case was extreme, it appeared the source of human psychological suffering was indeed a matter of the ego taking control and blocking out the spirit, like how a passing cloud blocks out the sunlight. Although Robert was filled with delusion and paranoia, he also had moments of clarity. Occasional rays of sunshine would get through his dark and turbulent mind.

I thought about the movie *A Beautiful Mind,* which tells the true story of John Forbes Nash, a mathematical genius challenged with schizophrenia. He overcame his illness by witnessing his thoughts and perceptions and then separated reality from illusion. It was his spirit that did the witnessing and determined what was true and what was false. He found a crack in the darkness of his mind to let a bit of light in. Although he did this without medication, I am not advocating for someone with serious mental health challenges to stop using medications. That should be a decision made with a mental health advisor. I do, however, believe as a society we rely too heavily on pills to tame the voice of the ego.

I remember when I bought my copy of the DSM at the campus bookstore. It was required reading for my graduate courses. I skimmed through it and noticed the section on grief. It stated that feelings of grief for longer than a year may be considered a mental illness that could be treated with medication. It had been over two years since Bob's death, and I still grieved. I thought, how can anyone decide how long we are allowed to grieve before we are labeled with a mental disorder? What about someone who is grieving over a lost job? How long can they grieve? Or someone missing a partner after a divorce or the end of a relationship? How long can they grieve? I felt a resistance to being labeled and classified for something that is a natural human reaction to a life-challenging event. Unfortunately, the system is set up where mental health providers are required to give a client a label and diagnosis rather than accept that life is messy, and grief is part of the human experience. Allen Frances, a past chair of the DSM task force said, "DSM diagnoses confuse mental disorder with the everyday sadness, anxiety, grief, disappointments, stress responses that are a part of the human condition."[20]

I wondered who decides what is considered a mental illness and how these labels come about, so I did a little research. I found that 69 percent of the decision-makers on the panel of the DSM have financial ties with pharmaceutical companies.[21] I also learned mental healthcare providers need to label their clients with a disorder found in the DSM before they can be paid by insurance companies.[22] It's advantageous for those involved to believe that normal sadness is an illness that needs to be treated with medication. We are led to believe we can shift from left-sided feelings to right-sided feelings with only a pill.

Even the United Nations cautioned us against an overreliance on happy pills to avoid unmasking the real problem. It put out this statement in 2017, "The present-day bio medical narrative of depression is based on the biased and selective use of research

---

20 "Conversations in Critical Psychiatry: Allen Frances, MD," Psychiatric Times, accessed October 24, 2022, https://www.psychiatrictimes.com/veiw/conversations-critical-psychiatry-allen-frances-md.
21 Cosgrove and Krimsky, "A Comparison of DSM-IV and DSM-5 Panel Members' Financial Associations with Industry: A Pernicious Problem Persists," PLOS Medicine, March 13, 2012, https://www.ncbi.nlm.nih.gov/pmc/articles/PMC3302834/.
22 "Diagnostic System Lacks Validity," Council for Evidence-Based Psychiatry, accessed October 24, 2022, http://cepuk.org/unrecognised-facts/diagnostic-system-lacks-validity/.

outcomes. The excessive use of medications and other biomedical interventions cause more harm than good, undermines the right to health and must be abandoned."[23] In many cases, it's our spirit that needs fixing and not our brain.

While it seemed this simple concept of "ego bad/spirit good" made total sense, I wondered if there is conclusive scientific evidence to back this up. I read about neuroscientists who work with a special kind of brain imaging, (functional magnetic resonance imaging [fMRI]), to observe the effect thoughts have on brain activity. They studied patterns of negative egoic thoughts that lead to anxiety and depression, as well as the positive thoughts of love, compassion, and gratitude. They found that levels of stress, depression, and anxiety were substantially reduced when participants focused on positive thoughts.[24] Connecting to the thoughts of the spirit also has a healing effect on our physical health. Neuroscientists have found emotions supported by spirituality such as hope, contentment, love, and forgiveness affect the neural pathways that connect to the endocrine and immune systems.[25] This improves blood pressure, cortisol levels, and concentration. Further studies have shown that people diagnosed with a mental illness not only find hope, meaning, and comfort in spirituality but are less likely to be addicted or suicidal.[26]

---

23 Karter, Justin, "United Nations Statement Criticizes Medicalization of Depression on World Health Day," Mad in America, April 6, 2017, https://www.madinamerica.com/2017/04/united-nations-statement-criticizes-medicalization-depression-world-health-day/.
24 "Positive thinking: Stop negative self-talk to reduce stress," Mayo Clinic, February 03, 2022, https://www.mayoclinic.org/healthy-lifestyle/stress-management/in-depth/positive-thinking/art-20043950.
25 Vaillant, George E., "Positive Emotions, Spirituality and the Practice of Psychiatry," Mens Sana Monogr, December 2008, https://www.ncbi.nim.nih.gov.
26 K. Milner, P. Crawford, and M. Slade, "The experiences of spirituality among adults with mental health difficulties: a qualitative systematic review," May 2019, https://pubmed.ncbi.nlm.nih.gov/31046852/.

As time passed, my encounters with Robert became more frequent. During his brief moments of clarity, I learned what it's like to be homeless and challenged with schizophrenia. He told me people who passed by would occasionally spit on him or tell him to get out of town. Or both. He carried everything he owned on his back and in the small cart that he pushed around. I always stopped to chat with Robert when I saw him on the bench or in the nearby park, his second favorite place to pass the time.

One day while walking Otis in the park, I ran into Robert. He was sitting in the shade of a group of oak trees, talking to himself and flailing his arms about. The sight of Otis always calmed him down. They got into their throw-and-catch game while I watched and eventually fell asleep on the freshly mowed grass. I remember waking up surrounded by Robert, some of his homeless friends, and a tired Otis.

One of my neighbors from the condo happened to be walking by and looked concerned to see me lounging on the grass with Robert and the others. He gave my friends a disapproving look before nervously asking if I was okay. Was he thinking I was in some sort of danger? Was there something I should know but didn't get? I understood he most likely had some scary assumptions about my friends, but I wished he would have taken the time to get to know them for who they really were and let go of the fear of who he thought they were. Honestly, some of the wealthy people Bob worked with scared me more than these gentle souls.

Making assumptions is a common ego trap. It is filled with judgments and false beliefs. Many times, our assumptions lead to hurtful gossip and poor communication. We misunderstand people and situations for what they truly are. The spirit objectively asks questions and relies on fact. Again, it chooses truth over beliefs.

THE FIGHT INSIDE

I introduced Michele to Robert when she came to Reno for one of our sister visits. At the time, she was working as a public health nurse in San Diego. She had a deep empathy for the homeless and all vulnerable populations. We ran into Robert while walking through the park one day. She instantly took a liking to him and whenever she came to town, she would insist on taking Robert out for lunch.

We usually went to the same café around the corner from my condo, known for its friendly staff and simple menu. We always found a table near a window where we could keep our eyes on Robert's belongings that he had to leave outside.

Robert went out of his way to be polite to the server when it came time to order, but I noticed he kept his head down. The prolonged looks and whispers from the other customers perhaps made him feel uncomfortable.

Michele was present in her conversations with Robert even if they included his paranoid delusions. She went along with whatever craziness he was sharing and the two of them would either become silent and serious or burst into laughter. The more people stared, the louder Michele got. She also made sure Robert ordered two of his favorite burgers with extra fries and had the server wrap up what he didn't finish to take with him. Robert loved her visits and always asked about her after she left.

I met other homeless men like Robert when I interned at the homeless resource center who were challenged with schizophrenia. A few lucky ones were able to get help after being on a waiting list for sometimes many months. A case manager would see that they had access to the right meds, food, and a bed. Stability for their mind and body. Basic human needs that most of us take for granted. Unfortunately, due to a lack of available housing and services, many never make it to the top of the list and are doomed to a life that struggles to survive each day.

MAMA SUNSHINE

I met several of these survivors at the homeless resource center. One day while approaching the entrance to the center, I was greeted by a client I hadn't seen in a while. Her name was Shirley, known as Mama Sunshine around town. She was often seen panhandling or collecting empty cans to scrape up enough money for a forty-ouncer and some rollies, which are hand-rolled cigarettes. She told me she had just been released from jail after purposely throwing a brick through a convenience store window. She said she had been seriously suffering from a toothache for weeks and figured her only chance of seeing a dentist would be in jail.

After she waited for the cops to come, she gladly put her hands out to be cuffed and off she went to get her tooth pulled. She also enjoyed the additional bonus of a place to sleep and a hot meal. I found her idea to be creative and couldn't help but be impressed. It also made me wonder how, as a society, we have forced the least fortunate to commit crimes to get the healthcare they need. This is truly messed up.

HOUSING FIRST

Reno was struggling like every other city in the country to solve the homeless crisis. The number of Americans living without homes, in shelters, or on the streets is on the rise.[27] In Reno, you couldn't ignore the increased number of tent camps popping up around town or the many people lining up in parks patiently waiting for a plate of

---

[27] Woodruff, Judy, and Cuevas, Karina, "What's behind rising homelessness in America?" PBS, December 28, 2021, https://www.pbs.org/newshour/show/whats-behind-rising-homelessness-in-america.

food served by a local community group. I had a hard time sleeping, particularly on cold and rainy nights, thinking about these people huddled in tents, doorways, or under a sheet of cardboard, doing their best to stay warm and dry. I soon became involved with community advocacy groups to help find a solution.

In the fall of 2016, a year after we opened the drop-in center, the city sent me to a Housing First conference in Los Angeles to learn what other cities are doing and report back my findings. I learned about the Housing First model, which is an evidence-based solution to homelessness. It provides them with a place to live along with supportive services without the strict condition of mandatory sobriety.

The National Alliance to End Homelessness has found that most clients who take part in the optional supportive services experience greater housing stability.[28] Clients are more likely to participate in job training programs, attend school, and discontinue substance use if they have a stable home. It's estimated that a Housing First program could cost up to $23,000 less per year for each homeless person than a shelter program.[29] I couldn't wait to learn more.

The conference was located only a couple blocks from the center of the infamous "Skid Row," an area that has a homeless population of between 4,200 and 8,000 living within a 2.7 square mile range.[30] I wanted to see for myself what this looked like, so I walked through it after the first day of the conference. I was alarmed to see how permanent the tent setups were that lined both sides of the streets. The smell of urine and garbage permeated the air as I passed through a maze of tents, propane camp stoves, fire pits, piles of trash, and

---

28 "Housing First," National Alliance to End Homelessness, March 20, 2022, https://endhomelessness.org/resource/housing-first/.
29 "Housing First," https://endhomelessness.org/resource/housing-first/.
30 "Skid Row, Los Angeles," Wikipedia, accessed October 24, 2022, https://en.wikipedia.org/wiki/Skid_Row,_Los_Angeles.

pieces of furniture that looked like they were pulled from a dump. All this lined both sides of the streets for several blocks.

As I continued down the street, I scoped the scene for someone I could talk to. I made eye contact with a thirty-something African American woman, sitting in a lounge chair next to her tent, semi-blocking the sidewalk. Her matted dreadlocked hair half-covered her rough and weathered face. I slowed my pace and smiled at her. She stared at me and with a wide smile that exposed a few decayed teeth she nodded. I stopped and introduced myself. As I looked closely into her eyes, I sensed a connection and a weird closeness. I was upfront with her about my curiosity about what was going on around us. I had so many questions. How long had she lived there? How did she end up there? Where does she pee? How does she cook? Is she afraid at night?

She introduced herself as Lacy and explained why she claimed her spot on the sidewalk about a year earlier when she found herself broke and homeless. She lost her job because she had a mental breakdown that a doctor later described as one of a series of bi-polar episodes. Without a place to go to for help, she ended up on "the Row." She lives day by day eating what is available at the rescue mission and spends her time visiting with the others whom she called her family. She said everyone looks out for each other, but you must constantly watch your back. Her tent had been robbed several times, and she'd been attacked more than once by those she called, "crazies on a binge." She said that without any restrooms on the street, she and the others use their poop buckets before they dump them out into the sewer drains. She relied on one of the churches as a place to get her water for cooking and to take an occasional shower.

Lacy became agitated as she told me about the cops who had recently done a sweep and were taking her friends' belongings and giving out tickets before they were stopped by a few community advocates. Luckily, the cops hadn't been back, but she was also upset that a couple of out-of-state mental hospitals had been "patient dumping" and leaving them there with barely anything for survival.[31]

I noticed as Lacy and I were talking, others were closing in and wanted to get in on the conversation. I figured these rugged-looking characters must be part of the family that she talked about. Soon after she introduced me, I felt it was my cue to head out when one stumbled and fell before offering me a hit off a joint. I graciously declined his hospitality before I thanked and hugged Lacy goodbye and headed back to my hotel.

* * *

The three-day conference began at 8 a.m. each morning with speakers from around the country. The first speaker said we are all spinning our wheels trying to manage the problem of homelessness with Band-Aids and a lot of failed policies. The simple answer to solve the problem is to provide housing along with supportive services. They showed charts and graphs that illustrated how this approach would be cheaper and wiser than spending taxpayer's money on shelters, detox centers, jails, and emergency room visits. If a homeless person had a stable home, they would be more likely to recover from addictions, take mental health medications, become healthier, and have an increased sense of well-being. They may even get a job and become well-intentioned citizens.

This logic hit home when I read the *New Yorker* article, "Million-Dollar Murray," written by Malcolm Gladwell.[32] Gladwell tells the

---

31 Kloczko, Justin, "Hospitals Are Dumping Mentally Ill Patients in Los Angeles' Skid Row," Vice, June 21, 2016, https://www.vice.com/en/article/yvezpv/hospitals-are-dumping-mentally-ill-patients-in-los-angeles-skid-row.
32 Gladwell, Malcolm, "Million-Dollar Murray," The New Yorker, February 5, 2006, https://www.newyorker.com/magazine/2006/02/13/million-dollar-murray.

story of Murray Barr, a homeless man who died on the streets of Reno in 2005. Gladwell investigated Murray's many visits to the shelter, jail, and the county hospital. He estimated that the city spent roughly a million dollars supporting Murray's life on the street. Setting Murray up in an apartment with services would have been cheaper and more humane. The solution is obvious, but resistance comes from a belief that providing the homeless with a roof over their head is only rewarding bad behavior.

I brought back everything I learned at the conference and presented my findings at a meeting with the mayor and various community leaders. They listened, but only time will tell if I was able to plant any seeds for a better way.

Several years had passed since I first met Robert sitting on the park bench. I continued to visit him and listened to his often-incomprehensible stories filled with paranoia and magical thinking. I began to worry when a week went by, and he was missing from the bench or in the park. Maybe he was testing out new places to pass the day. Two weeks passed with no sign of Robert, and by then someone else had claimed his spot on the bench. I asked around and felt my heart sink when I heard he died. No one seemed to know the details, but I figured he died alone. At first, I felt a heavy sadness that quickly turned into a peaceful knowing that Robert no longer had to deal with the destructive voice in his head or the harshness of the streets.

PART THREE

SOUL TO SOUL, NOT ROLE TO ROLE

SOUL, NOT
SOLE TO ROLE

CHAPTER ELEVEN

TANZANIA

"We are like islands in the sea, separate on the surface but connected in the deep."

WILLIAM JAMES

I always wanted to travel and see firsthand what the world was like. I remember as a young child, carefully studying the pages of the National Geographic magazines that came in the mail. My curiosity and imagination went wild when I dreamed about these exotic and distant places. I studied pictures of the people living in their cities and villages and marveled at how they lived. The definition of a tourist is someone who travels for pleasure, usually sightseeing and staying in a hotel. Yes, I wanted to travel, but I wanted to be a different kind of tourist. I was more interested in connecting with the people than seeing the sights. I wanted to meet locals who could show and tell me their true story, not the filtered version made for tourists. I wanted to meet these people and learn about their innermost fears, desires, and vulnerabilities. I wanted to understand our similarities and differences.

Four years before Bob's death, I took one of these trips. It was the winter of 2006, when Michele, Tim, and I were sitting in a crowded plane on our way to eastern Africa. We were excited to spend the next three weeks volunteering in Tanzania and ready to experience a world completely foreign to us. Michele and I had talked about volunteering out in the world for a long time. We knew we lived a privileged life in the U.S. and felt a need to proactively give back and help make a difference. We were nudged by our spirits. Africa, being the poorest continent in the world and a place with the greatest need, became our first choice.

Rather than going about this on our own, and with no knowledge of how or where to help, Michele found an international volunteer agency online, Cross Cultural Solutions, that listed several NGOs (non-government organizations) who were seeking volunteers. She called their headquarters in New York City and gave them a brief history of our skills and experience along with a request to work in Africa. They sent us applications and a description of the NGOs who needed help with their daily operations or with specific projects. Michele loved kids, so she requested to work in a rural elementary school. Tim opted to volunteer in a school for disabled children, and I chose to help in a hospice/orphanage for children with HIV/AIDS and tuberculosis. The agency also provided volunteers with a place to stay, meals, and transportation to and from their placements.

Our handbook arrived the next week with instructions on how to prepare for the trip which included getting our passports and visas in order and taking immunizations for typhoid, yellow fever, influenza, hepatitis A and B, tetanus, rabies, and malaria. They also sent us a list of what to pack and an abbreviated English/Swahili dictionary. A month later, we were on our way.

Our plane landed at the Kilimanjaro Airport outside of Arusha, Tanzania, in the early evening when darkness was setting in. As we made our way through baggage claim and out of the terminal, I was relieved to see a man holding up a sign that read, "Cross Cultural Solutions." He broke into a welcoming smile and waved as soon as he saw us. I'm sure it was easy for him to spot us. We were the only three wide-eyed and travel-wearied *wazungus*, or white people, in the crowd. He helped us with our bags while saying, "Hujambo, hello, hello," and guided us to the parking lot. We climbed into an old Land Rover and headed to the basecamp, which would be our home for the next three weeks. After an hour of driving in the dark on rough and dusty roads, we arrived at our destination.

The base camp resembled a mini compound of several cabins surrounded by a nine-foot security wall with one main building in the middle. As we unloaded our bags, we were greeted by the staff and taken to our rooms. The rooms were in small cinderblock cabins that each slept four volunteers. Tim would share a cabin with three other men while Michele and I were led to a cabin for women. Two sets of bunk beds with mosquito netting over each mattress were the only furniture in our room. Each cabin had its own bathroom with a sign on the door that read, "If it's yellow keep it mellow. If it's brown flush it down." We were told the water was in short supply and not safe to drink, so be quick in the shower and use bottled water for brushing our teeth. I was relieved that we had a flush toilet in the cabin because the handbook said to be prepared to use pit toilets and always carry our own toilet paper because it's considered a luxury item.

Michele and I introduced ourselves to our new roommates while we unpacked and settled in. Bonnie was in her twenties and from Alberta, Canada. She planned to travel to the Jane Goodall Institute in the Congo when our volunteer time was up. Nancy, also in her twenties, was from Rhode Island and taking time off between jobs to travel. It had always been her dream to come to Africa, see the sights, and volunteer. The four of us talked late into the night and woke to the sound of roosters crowing outside our window as the sun came up.

The early morning air was heavy with humidity and carried a faint smell of burning garbage. Michele and I met Tim and the other volunteers in the canopied dining area that was central to our cabins. A buffet-style breakfast was arranged on a long wooden table next to the kitchen and included a woven basket filled with flatbread called Chapati and bowls of sliced mangos, watermelon, plantains, and boiled eggs. While we ate and chatted with the other volunteers, I noticed the women, including Michele and I, all wore the required long skirts that covered the knees and tee shirts that covered our shoulders. The handbook suggested the more skin we covered, the better.

We finished breakfast and boarded a van that would take us to our placements. The driver pulled out onto the main road, which was narrow and rutted with a patchwork of potholes. I hardly blinked my eyes as I looked out the window. Several women walked barefoot on the side of the road while balancing bundles of branches or bunches of plantains on their heads. They were wearing tee shirts and skirts made of printed cloth that wrapped around their waist. I later learned these skirts are called kangas. I imagined how hard life must be for these women who go out and collect scraps of wood just so they can keep a fire going to cook for their families. We passed huts made of dried mud or homes constructed from cardboard with roofs made of tin and sticks. Scattered between these homes were small bonfires releasing clouds of thick dark smoke from burning garbage and tires.

Our bus slowed and stopped as each volunteer departed for their placements. Michele and Tim had already been dropped off when I noticed there were only two other women and myself left on the bus. We learned we were assigned to the same place, Saint Lucia hospice and orphanage. Valerie was from California and taking a break from college. Susan had taken time off from her nursing job in Canada. While we were getting to know each other, the bus driver pulled over to the side of the road and stopped. Without saying a word, the door swung open, and he pointed to our destination.

We stepped off the bus and walked down a muddy path toward the orphanage, hidden behind a grove of banana trees and overgrown ferns. It was a simple rectangular building made of clay bricks, surrounded by a dirt yard and wooden fence. We rang a cowbell hanging by the front door and stood silent with nervous anticipation. A woman dressed in a navy skirt and dingy beige top greeted us in Swahili and invited us inside. It took a few seconds for my eyes to adjust to the darkness before I could see a wooden table in the center of the room that was surrounded by several miniature plastic chairs. I assumed this was where the children ate their meals.

The woman said her name was Dobadina and she, fortunately, spoke English. She was the head nurse and eager to show us around and introduce her staff of three. It was noticeably quiet, and I wondered where the children were until I looked into a large room crammed with bunk beds. Some children were sleeping while others peeked at us through the mosquito netting that was draped over bare mattresses. The heat and humidity seemed to draw out the distinct smell of urine and bleach.

Dobadina brought us into a back room used to store household supplies and the children's clothing. The room was stifling hot with flies buzzing everywhere. I was surprised to see a frail woman lying on a thin mat in the corner. Dobadina informed us that the woman was terminal with HIV/AIDS and not expected to survive the week. She said part of our duties would be to help feed and bathe the woman until she passed. The woman opened her eyes and looked at us while moaning something in Swahili. Dobadina knelt and comforted her as she told her that we would be taking care of her and the children. She half smiled before she closed her eyes and dozed off.

We were sorting through the children's clothing and arranging them in a large closet when Dobadina was called to the outside gate. Apparently, a man dropped off his niece because he couldn't take care of her. The young girl's mother had died of HIV/AIDS a few days earlier and she needed a home. Dobadina agreed to take care of the girl who looked about seven or eight years old. She accepted a bag of the girl's belongings and led her into the room where we were sorting through the clothes.

Dobadina introduced the young girl as Mercy and told us to keep an eye on her while she went into town to pick up supplies. Mercy stood motionless with a frightened look on her face. She was barefoot and wearing an oversized torn dress that hung over her tiny and frail body. Her hair was shaved, which was the norm for both girls and boys. I could see her scant frame tremble as she stood there. To relieve her fear and anxiety, I smiled and began to sing a silly children's song I learned in Swahili from a YouTube video, but she remained wide-eyed and still.

As the days passed, I gave most of my attention to Mercy who tugged at my heartstrings, perhaps because I could still feel that scared nine-year-old girl in me when my own mother died years before. She slowly warmed up to me and reached for my hand whenever I was there.

The orphanage and entire neighborhood had no electricity or running water. The only available water came from a rusted hand pump in the backyard. Also in the backyard was a pit toilet that everyone used. One day, I noticed a cup on the kitchen counter that contained several toothbrushes with the brush side immersed in dirty water. When I asked Dobadina about it, she said an American had brought the toothbrushes and suggested the children use them before they go to bed. This made me cringe because I doubted there was any toothpaste and most of the children had tuberculosis.

Each day Valerie, Susan, and I filled a rusted metal tub with water we pumped from the well. The children stripped down and took turns standing in the tub while we washed each one with a rag and a scrap of soap. When we finished with the last child, we refilled the tub and hand-washed the children's clothes. The wet clothes were hung on a line strung between two acacia trees. The cooking was done in a dilapidated shed behind the house. Meals were prepared in a black iron kettle that sat over a firepit fueled by charcoal or wood. Before each mealtime, smoke billowed upward from the open shed door followed by the smell of ugali (porridge) seasoned with garlic and curry. We helped set up the dinner meal on the main table in the late afternoon before we returned to base camp.

One morning when we arrived to work, Dobadina asked if we wanted to join her on a hospice outreach visit to check on a terminally ill patient who was living on her own. We followed Dobadina a mile down a dirt trail that was overgrown with ferns and brush. As we walked, she told us HIV/AIDS had rapidly spread through Tanzania and devastated the country. Although it was her job to educate people on prevention, she felt overwhelmed. Polygamy was still practiced while safe sex was not. Another challenge was to confront the widespread belief that if a man contracts the disease he would be cured if he has sex with a virgin. She said it was not uncommon to see grown men waiting for the young girls outside of the local schools.

Hearing this, I thought how destructive the beliefs started by one or a few individuals can snowball into a tragic practice like this. The crazy thoughts of an individual can become a lot more powerful and harmful to the world when collectively supported and fueled by others.

The acceptance of rumors and conspiracy theories are examples of the collective ego. Remember that choosing beliefs over truth is a dangerous trap of the ego. The collective ego thrives when others join in to support a belief. The collective spirit is focused only on facts and the truth.

When we reached our destination, Dobadina introduced us to the woman who was losing her battle with HIV/AIDS while she lived alone in her hut made of clay. She was confined to a worn cot set a few inches off the hard-packed dirt floor. There was nothing else in the room but a fire pit and a few cooking utensils. We sat on the ground next to the woman, and I held her hand which felt limp and cold. She stared at me rarely blinking while I smiled and stroked her hand. Her breathing was soft and rapid as her frail chest expanded and contracted.

In the silence of the room, as we sat there looking at each other, the woman strained to say something to Dobadina that sounded like a whisper in Swahili. I looked at Dobadina and asked what she said. Dobadina replied, "She said you have peace in your face." Dobadina pulled a container of juice from her knapsack and lifted the woman's head to help her swallow. She softly spoke to the woman in Swahili and then stood up, which was our signal that it was time to leave. I gently squeezed the woman's hand before I let it go. While her gaze was still on me, I noticed her mouth barely smiled as I released her hand. Valerie, Susan, and I stood up and followed Dobadina outside. The connection I felt with this dying stranger can only be described as soul to soul. A simple human-to-human moment that I have always treasured.

On the way back to St. Lucia, Dobadina abruptly stopped and pointed to a mound of dirt by the side of the path. She told us she recently buried a patient there, after borrowing a shovel from a neighbor. I looked at the mound with nervous curiosity, hoping I wouldn't see a leg or arm sticking out. I didn't.

Back at base camp, Michele, Tim, and I compared our stories of the day. Michele teared up as she spoke about an albino child at the school who was shunned by the other students because of his pale skin and white hair. The teachers were concerned that he would be killed for his body parts because some of the witch doctors in the community used albino body parts in their magic potions. She also talked about how hard it was to watch the teachers routinely hit the kids during class. Corporal punishment was legal in the schools. Her instinct was to step up and say something, but she knew she had to bite her tongue and let go of her cultural judgments. We weren't in Kansas anymore.

Tim told of going with the special needs teacher to visit a disabled boy who was confined to his home. The child couldn't move his lower body and wheelchairs were too expensive which made them impossible to come by. He lived in a typical one-room mud hut with his mother and father. Inside was a wooden table, three stools, and a cooking fire in the corner. Each of the family members slept on a piece of woven material they rolled out onto the dirt floor at night. Tim said that when he and the teacher arrived, the boy used his upper body to drag himself across the floor to greet them. He burst into a huge smile and beamed when he saw the teacher.

After dinner that evening Tim, Michele, and I sat quietly on the back porch behind the kitchen. We could hear dishes clanging, crickets chirping, and the cheerful voices of the cooks who were cleaning up from dinner and prepping for the next morning's breakfast. Although no one spoke, I knew we all felt an uneasy sense of guilt mixed with gratitude for living such a privileged and abundant life, while so many others suffer horribly and go without. It seemed wrong and unfair.

Michele, Tim, and I decided to spend our first free weekend in Zanzibar, an island off the eastern coast of Africa. Getting there would require a quick flight, so we arranged for a ride to the airport. As we drove along the main road, our driver pointed out Mount Kilimanjaro off in the distance. It had been too dark to see it when we first arrived in Tanzania a couple of weeks earlier. But there it was, a solo mountain towering high into the clouds, surrounded by a vast African savannah. Our driver recalled his youth when the mountain stood brilliantly, covered in snow. Now, the melting glacier on the summit that supplied fresh drinking water to much of the country is expected to completely dissolve by 2040.[33] Recent wildfires on the mountain and drought have caused a migration of animals and people to flee the area. Rivers and streams that were once fed by the glacier have been drying up and making it harder or impossible for farmers to grow crops. I would have wanted to learn more from the driver, but we were at the airport just in time to make our flight.

We arrived in Zanzibar and checked into an Arabic-style hotel Michele had found online. The hotel was in central Stone Town, the old part of Zanzibar City, known for its exotic cultural heritage of Arabic, Persian, Indian, and European influences. The hotel lobby was spacious with high ceilings and stained-glass windows. The Islamic call to prayer broadcasted from rooftop loudspeakers echoed throughout. The hallway to our room had mosaic-tiled floors that were covered with thick ornate carpets. Our room had three single beds enclosed with mosquito netting and an arch-shaped window that overlooked the Indian Ocean. After we dropped our bags in the room, we left the hotel and walked through a maze of ancient narrow cobblestone streets lined with homes and shops, all with unique hand-carved wooden doors. The ancient doors were studded with sharp silver spikes which were used hundreds of years ago to keep aggressive elephants from entering.

We passed a stage in the town square that we learned had been an auction platform to buy and sell slaves. Apparently, Zanzibar was the hub of the east African slave trade in the nineteenth century. It is estimated that 600,000 slaves were sold on the island between 1830 and 1863.[34] The auction stage had the original shackles built into the

---

33 Ngugi, Brian, "Mount Kilimanjaro, Kenya, Rwenzori glaciers to disappear by 2040," The East African, October 20, 2021, https://www.theeastafrican.co.ke/tea/science-health/kilimanjaro-kenya-rwenzori-glaciers-to-disappear-by-2040-3589352.

34 Whitman, Mark, "Stone Town Zanzibar: From Exotic Spices, the Infamous Slave Trade to Artisan Mastery," Climb Kilimanjaro Guide, accessed October 24, 2022, https://www.climbkilimanjaroguide.com/stone-town-zanzibar/.

stone, and I imagined the horror these people must have felt standing on that stage about to be sold to the highest bidder.

We rode in a taxi boat to Prisoner Island and saw the caverns where slaves were kept before being packed into wooden ships and sent off to their destinations. While we walked around the castle-like structure and climbed down into underground cells with shackles lining the walls, I felt a thick and heavy energy within those stone walls. How is it possible that humans could treat each other like that? I knew it was the collective ego on full display, showing humans seeing others as non-human objects they could buy and sell, all in the name of power and greed. I also wondered why I never learned the truth about slavery in school. I remember being taught about the Civil War as if it were some romanticized conflict between northern whites and southern plantation gentlemen, *Gone with the Wind* style.

> *The collective deep wounds of racism have never been healed in the United States. Remember, you must honestly examine the wound before you can scrub it clean. Our nation has glossed over many historic facts because it can be unpleasant to face the truth. Burying the truth has caused racial tension that, when triggered, has sparked violent protests and terrorist acts. The only way to heal as a nation is to have an honest conversation about our racist culture and find compassionate ways to heal together. Only then will this buried heavy egoic energy be released.*

Three weeks after our stay in Africa, it was time to return to Truckee. Re-entry was a challenge while I tried to readjust to the rush and disconnection of daily life in America. As I stood in line at the local Starbucks, I could feel the anxiety and the separateness of people who were impatiently waiting for their expensive "mochafrapachinolattes." A woman in the pickup line kept insisting to the barista that her drink was taking too long. When her drink was ready, she rushed off in a huff without acknowledging or smiling at anyone. I couldn't help but think the amount she paid for her drink may have covered the cost of feeding everyone at St. Lucia for an entire day.

Global inequity is a symptom of the collective ego. The traps of greed, materialism, and viewing others as separate are reflected in our world where eight billionaires are wealthier than half the entire human population.

CHAPTER TWELVE

WALKING TREES

In July of 2011, Michele and I took a trip to Peru right after I graduated, and only a month before I laid the groundwork for Eddy House. Our destination was an eco-lodge located several miles deep into the Amazon River basin. We took a ten-seater plane from Lima to Puerto Maldonado which is at the mouth of the river and then planned to catch a boat to the lodge.

When we arrived in Puerto Maldonado, we dodged traffic and bicycles as we ran across the gravel road that connected the airport to the boat docks. I was told this was a quiet and sleepy fishing village, so I was surprised to see many people scurrying about amidst the sound of horns honking and noisy cars backfiring black puffs of smoke into the dusty air. We found our boat and climbed in. While waiting for more passengers to arrive, I asked the captain, who was wearing a wide-brimmed hat and faded rubber chest waders, what all the commotion was about. He told us gold mining, mainly illegal, had flooded the town with people hoping to get rich.

As we traveled down the river and away from town, we could see acres upon acres of open pit gold mines. The captain said this

THE FIGHT INSIDE

entire area used to be dense Amazon forest filled with wildlife. Now it was barren land covered with a grey liquid sludge made of toxic chemicals used to extract the gold. The captain went on to say the world is suffering because of deforestation. Moisture once stored in the trees formed clouds when it evaporated. The clouds provided rain to much of the world. Now, without the clouds and rain, much of the planet is experiencing severe drought conditions. Also, the forest used to absorb CO_2 from the atmosphere, but now for the first time, it is releasing more carbon than it is removing.[35] As the captain spoke, I thought about the drought in Tanzania that caused the snow to disappear on Mt. Kilimanjaro.

Man-made climate change reflects the collective ego. A belief that we are separate and superior to Nature comes from the ego. The shared values of greed and domination have put us at war with her. The collective spirit knows we are part of nature and not separate. When we try to conquer and destroy her resources, we are only harming ourselves into extinction.

Miles down the river, we pulled close to shore. The captain shut down the motor and pointed to a steep set of stairs barely visible through the thick jungle foliage. Michele and I took off our shoes, rolled up our pants, and climbed out of the boat. We waded through knee-high water toward a lengthy set of wooden stairs that led up a steep bank to the lodge. We later learned that stepping into the water was dangerous and risky because it's home to anaconda snakes and piranhas.

The lodge was two stories high and constructed of mahogany logs and planks strung together with rope and vines. Although it was built

---

35 Carrington, Damiam, "Amazon rainforest now emitting more CO2 than it absorbs," The Guardian, July 14, 2021, https://www.theguardian.com/environment/2021/jul/14/amazon-rainforest-now-emitting-more-co2-than-it-absorbs.

on the jungle floor, it looked like a giant tree house. We were told the designated times that the power would be on and to use the electricity sparingly. Charging a cell phone or a camera was okay but using a hairdryer or any other electrical gadget was prohibited. We walked across a swinging rope bridge that connected the main building to our room. The room had only three walls made of bamboo, which left one entire side of the room wide open to the jungle. The two beds had mosquito netting over them, but I couldn't help thinking, "What would prevent a snake or monkey to crawl in bed with me?" We nervously laughed about it as we did the "rock-scissors-paper" for the bed farthest from the open jungle. Michele won, so during our stay, I slept with the sounds of moving brush, howling monkeys, and unidentified creatures throughout the night.

During the day, we hiked in the humid and lush rainforest that seemed to be breathing and alive. Primordial ferns and enormous trees were playgrounds for colorful birds and energetic monkeys, reminding us of Jurassic Park. One of the staff members at the lodge pointed to a tree with extended and exposed roots and said that it had moved from one side of the lodge to the other side only within the past few years. This towering and thin tree is called a walking palm and constantly relocates itself to find better living conditions.

We met a couple from Seattle in the dining hall who told us about a shaman who lived about five miles down the river. They said he welcomes travelers at his home, and it is well worth a visit. They told us we could arrange for transportation at the front desk. We did, and after putting on complementary knee-high rubber boots, we waited for our ride by the river's edge.

We were greeted by a twentyish looking man standing in the middle of a hand-carved canoe using a pole to guide his way to the riverbank. He introduced himself as Raya while he pulled the canoe up onto the muddy bank. He wore a traditional native headband that matched his sweat-stained and faded tee shirt. He offered to be our guide for the rest of the afternoon and told us he was a local and could take us safely through the jungle trails that led to the shaman's home. We gladly accepted his offer after having visions of being lost in the rainforest.

While Michele and I sat in the unsteady canoe and slowly traveled down the river, I wondered what this shaman would be like. Would he have special powers that could heal any illness? Could he communicate with the otherworld and possibly bring me a message from Bob? I have heard of such things but never believed them. After getting out of the boat, Raya led us down a winding and narrow path toward the shaman's house.

We stopped at the intersection of three different trails and read a hand-carved sign that displayed an arrow and the word, "ayahuasca." At the end of the path, we could see a hut with a thatched roof surrounded by gardens and a large outdoor kitchen. A woman who recognized Raya invited us inside the open-aired hut where the shaman was chanting and sitting cross-legged on the floor in the middle of the room. He wore a headpiece covered with feathers and tassels. His thick wool robe partially covered his faded jeans and leather sandals.

We joined two other visitors who sat in front of him and listened to his stories, which Raya interpreted. He talked about the magic of the jungle and the powers of the plants, particularly the cappi vine and chacruna plant that he used to mix up a batch of ayahuasca. Michele and I knew ayahuasca was a brew with psychedelic qualities, like LSD. While we followed him outside to see his ayahuasca kitchen, we asked Raya if he had tried the shaman's ayahuasca. He described his last ayahuasca experience, which landed him on the roof for two days. He couldn't remember how he got up there, but said the sky opened and pulled his spirit to the heavens while leaving his body on the roof. Michele and I looked at each other when Raya's friend approached us with a tray of tiny wooden cups of ayahuasca. Michele reminded me that we had to catch our flight back to Lima early the next morning. We respectfully declined but with a great deal of reluctance.

Back at the lodge, we reminisced about our past LSD trips. Fortunately, we never had a bad one and experienced what seemed like a beautiful opening and expansion of our minds. We recalled having a feeling of total presence with everything. Our heightened senses made us see, feel, and hear everything on a different level as though we entered a new dimension or energy frequency. The experience of realizing these new perceptions caused a dramatic shift to the right side of the OHM scale. We joked that it should be put in the world's drinking water supply so everyone could have the experience. Perhaps then we would be inclined to take better care of each other and the planet.

It's interesting that recent studies have found psychedelics to have positive effects on PTSD, depression, and anxiety.[36] These compounds seem to quiet the voice of the ego down to a faint whisper while allowing the voice of the spirit to be heard loud and clear. In his book, *How to Change your Mind*, Michael Pollan describes the psychedelic experience as, "Ego dissolution, followed by love, and a spiritual sense of oneness. Once the experience is over, ego is back in uniform and on patrol. Fortunately, you now are aware of this other state of consciousness and can cultivate it." I interpret this statement as a call to keep the ego in check.

As I'm writing this, I recall a student I had when I taught a social work class at the University. He was a veteran named Don who decided to become a social worker after completing a few tours in Afghanistan. He lost his right leg during combat on his last tour. Don was stocky with a muscular build and sat quietly in the back of the room. During class, he would either scroll on his phone or give me

---

36 Villines, Zawn, "What to know about psychedelic therapy," Medical News Today, June 29, 2021, https://www.medicalnewstoday.com/articles/psychedelic-therapy.

the stink eye while I taught. He had an angry harshness about him that made me uncomfortable, but I learned to ignore his intense vibe.

A year later, I received an email from Don asking if we could meet for coffee. I was curious why he wanted to meet, so I said, "Of course." The Don who showed up was not the same angry student I remembered. A warm smile replaced his intense scowl, and he beamed with exhilarated contentment. He was eager to tell me about an experimental program he participated in to relieve his PTSD. It included taking ayahuasca. He said the experience took him deep into the moment the explosion took his leg. He faced his trauma head-on and let it go. He said he felt as though a heavy boulder that had been chained around his neck was suddenly gone. His heart opened to a sense of love and oneness which he still embraces.

Based on what Don told me and through my own experiences, I am convinced psychedelics have a way of directly tapping into the spirit. While I fully believe in the benefits of psychedelics, I also know there is a risk involved if you are not in the right mindset or if the setting feels threatening. Don's experience was with a guide who safely and successfully helped him along the way.

CHAPTER THIRTEEN

LOST AT SEA – LOST ON LAND – GREECE

It was the spring of 2017 when Michele called late one night from her home in Atlanta. She had been watching stories on the news about overloaded boats filled with refugees escaping their war-torn homes in Syria, Iraq, and Afghanistan. Tragically, many didn't survive the treacherous waters and their bodies washed up on the shores of Greece and Italy. I'd seen the same news reports. The horrific images of lifeless children floating face down in orange life jackets were stuck in my mind. Michele contacted Cross Cultural Solutions and found they were looking for volunteers to help with programs they were setting up in several refugee camps in Greece. Eddy House had been open for six years and was running strong with a great staff and executive director. It was no longer necessary for me to be involved with daily operations, so it was easy to clear my calendar.

THE FIGHT INSIDE

Only two weeks after that call, Michele and I arrived at the Athens airport, where we met other volunteers who traveled from different parts of the world. We boarded a van and were driven to our base camp by our volunteer leader, Mohammad. He had been the agency's volunteer director in Morocco and was now assigned to oversee the refugee program in Greece.

It was late in the day when we arrived at our hotel, located in the small coastal town of Chalkida, an hour away from the refugee encampments. Early the next morning, the staff briefed us on what to expect and gave us a condensed cultural education that explained middle eastern social and cultural norms. We were told to dress modestly with tops covering our shoulders and shorts covering our knees. We also should not hug or touch anyone, especially the women. They warned us that many of the refugees had experienced severe trauma and could be emotionally triggered; therefore, we were to keep the conversations light.

One of the staff members described her experience greeting the refugees when the boats first landed on the shores of Lesbos, a Greek island about ten miles off the coast of Turkey. The refugees, crammed into inflatable rafts, landed in Lesbos after crossing the Aegean Sea. Turkish smugglers arranged the trip which usually took place in the dark of night to avoid detection. She described the times she was pulled under water amid the frenzy and panic while assisting them out of the boats and onto land. Many of the refugees were in shock after witnessing a loved one tragically lost overboard.

The orientation ended, and we boarded a bus headed to a camp called Ritsona. When we arrived, we passed through a security gate before the bus came to a full stop. I could see rows of portable units lined up in a condensed area that stretched for at least a mile. Children played in the narrow spaces between the structures while a few women gathered over communal cooking fires. This camp, which was set up as a humanitarian effort to provide comfort and safety for more than 900 Syrian and Afghan refugees, felt like a drab military complex surrounded by rusted barbed wire.

A man dressed in camo fatigues and flashing a wide smile that exposed several missing teeth approached our group. He introduced himself as the camp commander and was eager to show us around. Mohammad and the commander led us down a muddy road, passing the FEMA-style portables mixed in with military-grade tents. When we passed a stone building that served as a communal latrine, the commander stopped and warned us not to wander off into the brush where dangerous snakes and wild boars were plentiful.

Mohammad summoned our group together and assigned our duties. Michele was happy to assist with the children, and I was asked to be part of a vision program. He asked a woman standing near me to also help with the vision program. Her name was Laurie and she had traveled alone from her home in Kansas City to volunteer. Like Michele and me, she was motivated by what she saw and heard on the news. Mohammad led us to a separate portable unit where we would perform vision screenings and determine which residents may need glasses. Multiple boxes of used reading and prescription glasses had been donated by a nonprofit in England.

After Mohammad gave Laurie and me a brief training, we set up the room and opened the door. Children and adults had gathered outside and were eagerly waiting to be seen. The children giggled while we measured their height and weight and checked their vision. Mohammad interpreted while I asked them to cover one eye as I held up a chart about five feet in front of them. The chart displayed rows of arrows that went from large to small. They told me how many arrows they could see and what direction they pointed to. Laurie entered the results into a computer program that let us know which type of glasses would improve their sight. The adults were somber but expressed gratitude as they went through the line. When we were

THE FIGHT INSIDE

able to match someone with the proper glasses, their response was filled with gratitude and excitement.

Michele and I reconnected at the end of the day and compared stories. She said some of the children's behavior reflected the past trauma they had experienced. Many screamed when volunteers coached them to play in a small plastic swimming pool filled with water. Getting into the water must have reminded them of their treacherous journey. She also found several dolls in the toybox missing their heads. When she brought that up to the commander, he said they were mimicking the beheadings they witnessed at home.

The next day, Michele went back to Ritsona, but Laurie and I were assigned to set up the vision program at another camp located near the town of Oinofyra. The camp was in an abandoned chemical factory that had been empty for years. The inside of the dilapidated building was partitioned into makeshift tiny cubicles that each housed a family. The cubicles were spaces about six-foot by six-foot with walls built of thick cardboard and thin sheets of plywood. You could tell the size of the families by how many pairs of shoes were left by their door.

Laurie and I found it hard to communicate with the residents because most spoke Arabic, Farsi, or Pashto. I was happy to meet a teenage boy named Amir, who was fluent in English. He was tall for his age and dressed in dirty, grey, loose pants and a tattered Red Sox tee shirt. He told me he had been at the camp for almost a year after leaving his war-torn village in Syria. His eyes welled with tears when I asked if his family was with him. He answered no but wished to join his mother and two brothers someday. He was separated from his family during their escape from the bombings and destruction. He was happy his family had made their way to Germany even though it was without him. He was losing hope of getting permission to join his family because the asylum office has been closed for a long while. No one knew when it would open again.

Amir became my new best friend and interpreter, as he introduced me to others. I now had the opportunity to hear some of the residents' stories and to learn about their backgrounds. I knew I had to be careful not to stir up unresolved strong emotions, so I tried to keep it polite and superficial. I was surprised by how eager they were to tell their stories, which I sensed was a way that helped them process. Again, I was reminded of the power of just listening.

Many of the adults I met were professionals and well-educated. Some were doctors, teachers, or attorneys back in their home country. I noticed their eyes light up when I asked them to describe the country they came from. One elderly man reminisced about the rolling hills and fruit trees that surrounded his home in Afghanistan. His eyes became misty, and his voice cracked as he spoke, which made it obvious that he missed his past life.

Many described the horrific devastation and violence they witnessed in the towns they fled. The constant bombings and lack of food and services forced them to leave. Escaping was their only option to stay alive and protect their family, and they were grateful to find safety but were now faced with surviving in an unfamiliar country and unable to get documentation to work or move on. The border closings and bureaucratic backlog of asylum applications made it impossible to schedule a hearing date. They felt powerless, and it became a reality that their life was destined to stay in the camps indefinitely with little or no hope for the future.

I wondered how this humanitarian crisis happened and learned that in 2016, the EU made a deal with Turkey to curtail the flow of desperate refugees coming over the northeastern Greece/Turkey border from Syria.[37] While the refugees were blocked from crossing

---

[37] Cook, Lorne, and Fraser, Susan, "EU greenlights major funding plan for refugees in Turkey," AP News, June 25, 2021, https://apnews.com/article/lebanon-middle-east-turkey-europe-migration-e9395d4a3376e8d53cd8a51508fc4a61.

the border on land to Greece, they took their chances coming across the sea. Amir and refugees like him are now trapped in a country that doesn't want them. Although I wished the camp provided the compassion and resources the refugees needed, I understood that Greece couldn't give them this support but did its best. Greece had problems of its own. The country was bankrupt at that time, and the rest of the world wasn't willing to help.

When it came time to return home, I felt a sense of guilt and privilege for having the freedom to leave this hopeless place. I understood I was no different from my new friends and would have done whatever it took to survive and seek safety for myself and my family. Just as they did. While I understood we don't get to choose where we are born in life, I felt an obligation to not forget about the millions of humans suffering around the world who weren't as lucky as me. Many more will have to leave their homes as resources become scarce and conflicts erupt. I can only hope countries unite in a global effort to address the drivers of forced migration whether it's climate change, extreme poverty, or government corruption. Albert Einstein said, "We cannot solve our problems with the same thinking we used when we created them." Problems only arise from the collective ego. Solutions can only be found through the collective spirit.

> *Remember, the ego wants us to fear and feel separate from the other. It lacks compassion and empathy while it views the other as threatening. The tribalistic nature of the collective ego promotes nationalism and views the other as them vs. us. The collective spirit sees the other as no different from ourselves. We are all part of the human family with the same wants and needs. No one should suffer. We are all in this universal soup together and when one hurts, we all hurt, and when one rises, we all rise.*

Michele and I planned our return flight home to allow for five days in Rome. We stayed in a hotel located a few blocks from St. Peters Square in Vatican City and close to the Coliseum. On our first day in Rome, we woke early and set out to see the sites. When we toured the grounds of Vatican City, it was obvious that the Catholic Church is the richest organization in the world.[38] Priceless artwork and ornate architecture covered the grounds. We later walked a short distance to the Coliseum, where gladiators once fought and human sacrifices to the gods were performed.

While exploring the ancient amphitheater, I thought about how religion and culture have evolved over time. Religious believers used to worship mythical gods who threw lightning bolts down from the heavens. The concept that sinners would burn in hell for eternity originated back in 700 AD.[39] Putting the fear of God in the minds of people has been used as a way to gain power and control over the masses for centuries. The origins of most religions were rooted in love and compassion but evolved into a fear-based doctrine of "My god is better than your god." Kings and religious leaders have been worshiped and wars have been fought in the name of religion. While many find comfort in religion, today's statistics show a trend among young people moving away from the dogma of organized religion and toward a personal spiritual practice that feels right for them,[40] as well as a stronger connection and respect for Mother Nature and each other. This collective sense of oneness, acceptance, and inclusion brings hope for the future.

---

38 "The Catholic Church is the Biggest Financial Power on Earth," Zubeida Jaffer, accessed October 25, 2022, https://www.zubeidajaffer.co.za/the-catholic-church-is-the-biggest-financial-power-on-earth/.

39 "Hell," Wikipedia, accessed October 25, 2022, https://en.wikipedia.org/wiki/Hell.

40 "More Young People Are Moving Away From Religion, But Why?" NPR, January 15, 2013, https://www.npr.org/2013/01/15/169342349/more-young-people-are-moving-away-from-religion-but-why.

CHAPTER FOURTEEN

GHANA

In March of 2018, a year after my trip to Greece, Laurie and I planned to meet in Ghana to continue our work with the vision program. I boarded the plane and noticed I was the only white person on the flight. I thought how this must be what is normal for a person of color in Reno, which according to the latest census is 75 percent white. I stumbled down the aisle and found my seat next to a smiling Ghanaian man. Once seated, he leaned over and offered a friendly handshake while he introduced himself as Abeeku. This introduction started a conversation that didn't end until nine hours later when we landed. He told me he was heading home after visiting a relative in the United States. He was very charming, personable, well-dressed, and not bad looking.

I tried to stay nonjudgmental when he said he founded an Evangelical Charismatic Church in Accra, the capital city of Ghana. He was very proud that his preaching made him extremely wealthy. He said it was easy money, and many of his friends wanted in on the action. He went on to say he had five wives and a few girlfriends on the side. In addition, he had many children with all his women but wasn't sure how many. He figured maybe seventeen or eighteen. By the time we landed, I had pretty much learned all that I wanted to know about this man. He was a hustler who was cashing in on the Evangelical Charismatic Church movement that started in the United States and began sweeping across Africa. This so-called prosperity movement is led by self-proclaimed pastors who pressure their followers to turn over financial offerings to be recognized and rewarded by God. On the flip side, if you didn't contribute, you would be punished by God. These false prophets are very successful at becoming incredibly wealthy and powerful all around the world.

We landed and as we parted ways, he handed me his information on a business card and said he hoped I would look him up during my stay in Ghana. I jokingly asked if he was looking for another wife or girlfriend. He suddenly had a serious look on his face and told me I would do fine with the other wives and girlfriends. I thought, yeah, no!

I was picked up at the airport by two Ghanaian men who drove me to the base camp in the village of Hohoe. The base camp was a single-story yellow stucco building with dark walls and concrete floors inside. The rooms were sparsely furnished, and the kitchen displayed rusted pots and pans hanging from the ceiling. The bedroom had several bunk beds covered in mosquito netting and a cabinet for volunteers to store their personal belongings. Laurie and three other volunteers, who had arrived earlier, were out exploring the town. When they returned, it was great to reconnect with Laurie and meet the others that included a couple from Atlanta and a woman from southern California. We gathered at the dining room table and talked over a meal of goat kabobs and fufu (a sticky rice made of yucca plants) before we turned in for the night.

The next morning, we were invited to attend a Sunday service in the village center. Inside the church, it was standing room only and stifling hot. Men, women, and children sang and danced to loud music that blared from giant speakers set on a stage. Suddenly, two men appeared out of the crowd and jumped onto the stage. They were dressed in bright red robes and began passing a basket around while yelling at the parishioners, "Give to God." I thought of Abeeku as I watched these dirt-poor people give up their crumbs of subsistence to a couple of guys who parked their new shiny black Land Rovers inconspicuously behind the church. It seems there are no limits to what people will pay for a sense of hope or a place in heaven. Unfortunately, there are opportunists ready to sell both.

We spent our days at the village school offering vision screenings for the students and teachers. When we arrived at the school each morning, several excited and barefoot children ran to the van waving and chanting "Hello, hello, hello." Most of the children were dressed in tattered mustard-colored shirts and brown shorts, which was the school uniform. Many of their shirts were missing most or all the buttons and their shorts were ripped and torn which made them almost impossible to wear. On our last day at the school, we showed up with sewing needles and spools of thread and went to work. The children stripped down to their underwear and lined up with excitement while waiting to hand over their desperate-looking garments. It was dark by the time we finished and returned to base camp. We must have patched close to one hundred uniforms. It was a successful day.

On my day off, I walked into Hohoe to check out the town. I stopped at a sidewalk cafe and ordered a coffee before I sat at a table near a distinguished-looking elderly man. He was dressed in a bright red and gold African print smock with matching pants. A short brimless cap half covered his grey-speckled hair. I was drawn to him with curiosity and wanted to know his story, so I made eye contact and smiled. He smiled back, which I took as an opening to start a conversation. I said, "Excuse me, sir, I'm traveling through and wonder if you could tell me about your country?" He broke into a wide smile and nodded. I scooched my chair closer to his table and unloaded my questions. What is the history of the area? What could he tell me about the local culture? What are his thoughts about the future of Ghana?

He introduced himself as Kwame and said he came from many generations of farmers who grew corn and yams on their family farm outside of town. While this man talked, his voice cracked as he told me the lure of western culture, with its values set on owning things like cell phones and the latest Jordans, has tempted the youth to leave the family farms and businesses to seek out the "hustle" in the city. His eyes teared up when he said his own two sons had left home for a future, he believed, destined for crime or some scheme that promised fast money. This exodus of youth was impacting the survival of the small villages that relied on the younger generation. He asked, "Who will be there to carry on with our farm?" He said this was never a question in the past. He went on to blame western culture for infecting the entirety of Africa with the destructive values of greed and materialism. I could sense the despair and fear this man felt as he thought about his own future and the future of his country.

He also talked about the influx of illegal gold miners who had taken over his neighbors' properties and threatened to dig on his own land. He said he complained to the local authorities but was ignored. He believed they were silent because they were paid off by the mining companies. He said the chemicals used by the miners had poisoned his family's drinking water and were killing his crops.

As he spoke, I thought of the deforestation and destruction Michele and I witnessed in Peru that was caused by illegal gold mining. I also remembered a past trip I had taken to Belgium. While at a museum in Brussels, I noticed a large photograph on the wall that showed many African men, women, and children lined up in a field with no hands. The information card below the photo described a time when the African people were forced to work on rubber plantations and if they didn't reach their daily harvesting quota, they would have their hands cut off. This was a clear example of the collective ego promoting power and greed. I thought of a quote from Jimmy Hendrix, "When the power of love overcomes the love of power, the world will know peace." I wondered if that would ever happen.

Kwame and I talked for about three hours before I realized I had to get back to base camp before darkness settled in. When I stood to leave, he hugged and thanked me for listening. As I walked back, Kwame's story of youth leaving for the hustle in the city played in my head. I remembered the time when Bob and I decided to give up our dream to live a simple life in Maine for the chance to climb the ladder of success in Boston. I wished I had a magic wand to go back in time to reverse that decision. I wondered if Bob would still be here if we had stuck with our original plan.

CHAPTER FIFTEEN

BLUE ZONES

My exposure to different people and cultures around the world left me asking what it means to live a good life? And how can some of the poorest people seem to be the happiest and most loving? In the fall of 2018, while volunteering in a rural area of Costa Rica, I was fortunate to meet some of these happy people living a good life.

Laurie and I met in a quiet village a few miles north of the city of Santa Cruz. We were there to continue our work with the vision program in the local schools. On our first day off, Franklin the program director, invited us to attend a dance performance in the small farming town of Hojancha, on the Nicoya Peninsula. When we arrived at the town square, we were welcomed by a group of teenagers who were wearing costumes representing their cultural heritage. The girls wore white ruffled blouses and brightly colored full skirts. Their hair was braided and accented with flowers. The boys wore wide-brimmed hats with bright red kerchiefs tied around their necks. A sash, wrapped around their waist, matched their kerchiefs. They gathered around us beaming with bright smiles and asked us to stay and watch their performance. We settled on a park bench in front of the outdoor community stage and watched them spin and stomp their heels to merengue music.

When the dancing stopped, they hopped off the stage and ran over to us. One of the boys introduced himself as Carlos and said he and the others were happy we were there. He said Hojancha didn't have many visitors, but it's a very special day when strangers become new friends. I was overwhelmed by the sense of love and joy they expressed with each other and with us. They held each other's hands while exuding a radiant energy that couldn't be ignored. I asked Carlos, "What makes you so happy?" He silently paused for a moment and replied, "If I am not feeling so happy, I will go see my friend and that will make me happy. And if I meet a friend who is not happy, I will help to cheer him up. That also makes me happy." He added that it was most important to take care of his family and friends no matter what was going on. As he spoke, I thought about the communities back home where loneliness, depression, and anxiety prevail. I wondered how they have it so right while we have it so wrong.

On the drive back to basecamp, Franklin told us that Hojancha was one of only five "blue zones" in the world.[41] He described "blue zones" as places where people live the longest and are the happiest people on earth. Many elders in these towns are well over one hundred years old. What the residents in these zones have in common is a strong sense of community and a relaxed and healthy lifestyle. They eat a predominately plant-based diet, and their food is locally and organically grown. The elders help to look after the children, and everyone respects and takes care of the elders. I realized that these areas are an example of the collective spirit reigning over the collective ego.

---

41 "Blue Zone," Wikipedia, accessed October 25, 2022, https://en.wikipedia.org/wiki/Blue_zone.

Unfortunately, there are only a few of these special places in the world where happiness thrives. It makes sense that the rest of the world is struggling and depressed when our systems fail to meet our spiritual needs of connection and purpose. Over the last thirty years, the number of Americans who claim to have no close friends has dramatically increased.[42] We scroll on social media looking for likes as if we're micro-dosing our validity. While green spaces are disappearing, we live like caged animals in a concrete jungle disconnected from nature. The existential threat of climate change and pandemics make it hard to find hope for the future. Many of the causes of depression aren't found in our biology but in the way we live. The truth is our political, social, and economic systems are starving our spirits while feeding our egos.

I went to my bunk that night and wondered if humans can come together and build a global society that benefits everyone. These thoughts led me to pull up the song "Imagine" from my playlist. I drifted off to sleep listening to John Lennon sing about such a world and calling on other dreamers to join in to make it happen.

* * *

I picked up many lessons while I traveled and met people from different cultures and backgrounds. I learned we all want the same things in life such as happiness, good health, safety, and connection. Whether a kid at Eddy House, a river guide in Peru, an orphan in Tanzania, an elder in Ghana, a teenager in Costa Rica, or a refugee in Greece, these are universal truths for all humans no matter where they live or their culture. There is truth in the quote from Rumi, "When I look at you, I see myself." I also learned a smile and showing

---

42 Cost, Ben, "Americans have fewer friends than ever before: study," New York Post, July 27, 2021, https://nypost.com/2021/07/27/americans-have-fewer-friends-than-ever-before-study/.

a little compassion is a cross-cultural way to cut through the bullshit. Afterall, we are all just humans doing the best that we can.

I recently heard a politician say we are about to lose the soul of our country and perhaps the world. I put together this Collective Open-Heart Mindfulness Scale as an indicator of how strong or weak our collective spirit is.

COLLECTIVE OPEN HEART MINDFULNESS SCALE
→

FEAR	1	2	3	4	5	LOVE
WAR						PEACE
NATIONALISM						GLOBALIZATION
EXPLOIT RESOURCES						RENEW RESOURCES
TRIBALISM						ONENESS
CENTRALIZED POWER						DECENTRALISED POWER
ORGANIZED RELIGION						OPEN SPIRITUALITY
PROFIT FOCUSED INVESTMENTS						SOCIALLY REPONSIBLE INVESTMENTS
PRIVILEGE						EQUALITY
MONEY CENTERED						HUMAN CENTERED
EXCLUSION						INCLUSION
GOOD FOR FEW						GOOD FOR ALL
WASTE RESOURCES						SUSTAIN RESOURCES

It seems we are literally at a tipping point and must ask ourselves: do we go left on the scale and realize the destruction of our planet and species? Or do we go right on the scale with a vision of a flourishing world that benefits all? The goal should be to create an environment that aligns with the values and needs of the spirit. There is a collective hunger to make these changes while people are starving for connection, fair and equitable institutions, and a healthy and thriving planet that everyone can call home.

* * *

I certainly don't know the answers to thriving in this world together; in fact, there seems to be more questions than answers. However, I believe that Mother Nature holds all the secrets and can guide us in the right direction if we allow her to do that. We know that within the nature of the universe there are endless complex systems from our own human body to the infinite cosmos, all living in harmony. Albert Einstein once said, "Look deep into nature, and then you will understand everything better." It is no longer survival of the fittest but survival of fitting together.

I sometimes imagine how beautiful the world would look if every human learned to tame their ego and live in their true spirit. Norman Vincent Peale said, "Change your thoughts and you can change the world." Remember that your thoughts determine your choices, actions, and how you live your life. If all humans kept their thoughts on the right side of the scale, this micro experience would collectively be brought to the macro level. Gandhi knew this when he said, "Be the change you want to see in the world."

CHAPTER SIXTEEN

SHEDDING THE EARTH SUIT

I was sitting on a stump taking off my hiking boots when my cell phone rang. It was Michele. Almost two years had passed since we took our trip to Greece, but we talked at least twice a week. I could hear her voice on the other end saying her usual, "Hey sis, how are you?"

I had just gotten back to my car after hiking one of my favorite trails. It was in early March of 2019, and there were still patches of frozen snow and ice scattered along the trail. I told her about the hike and didn't have any real updates on my life since the last time we talked. She said she had some news she had to tell me. Signals went off in my head that something was wrong. She spoke with hesitation as her voice became serious and said, "I was having back problems and pains in my stomach, so I went to the doctor. He did a scan and said I have stage 4 pancreatic cancer and three months to live."

I don't remember much of my drive home except trying to focus on the road through my tears. Michele lived in Atlanta with her husband

and near her three daughters and four grandchildren. I immediately quit my teaching job at the University and booked myself on a plane to Georgia. Andrea left her home in Phoenix, Arizona, to join me without hesitation, as we sisters have always been there for each other, no matter what.

When we arrived in Atlanta, we headed straight to the hospital where Michele had been admitted. When we walked into her room, she was sitting up on her bed smiling and reaching to us for hugs. She looked thinner than she did the last time I saw her six months earlier. Her face was pale and looked deflated. Her cheeks were sunken and hollow. The sparkle in her eyes was replaced with a dull and yellowish tinge.

Rather than let my fear and sadness take hold, I used humor to deflect these feelings that were surfacing. I said, "Hey sis, you'll do anything for attention. Why does it always have to be about you?" We laughed and then sank into the seriousness of it all as she updated us on her condition. She said her doctor sent her to the ER when she had trouble breathing. They discovered a pulmonary embolism, which was a blood clot in her lung. She was put on blood thinner medication and told to rest while they monitored her condition.

A few days after she was released from the hospital, the two of us found time to be alone in her bedroom. Her husband Mike was downstairs in the kitchen working on his laptop. The house was quiet. We sat on the floor while she sorted through piles of medical paperwork she had spread out around her. She suddenly stopped organizing the papers and said, "Sis, what do I do? The doctors told me I must make a choice to either start on chemo treatments that could maybe give me a little extra time or I could forget it and have hospice help me go out as comfortably as possible. What do I do?"

I couldn't find words because I didn't have an answer. While she waited for me to respond, she said, "I'm not afraid to die, but I don't know if I'm brave enough to fight. The only reason to take the chemo treatment would be to maybe live a couple extra months to see Mindy's baby."

Her daughter Mindy was six months pregnant. I drew a deep breath and said, "I can't tell you what to do, but if you decide to fight, I'm there as your biggest cheerleader, and if you choose to let go, I'll be close by your side. But one thing I know is, you are brave. You've pulled off some badass moves in your life."

She grabbed my hand and squeezed it before she jokingly said, "Sis, we've both done some badass shit, but you know how much I hate to puke. I don't mind losing my hair, but I don't want to puke." A few days later, she told her doctor she was ready to try the first of three rounds of chemo. She managed through the first infusion and fortunately didn't have the nausea she expected.

Despite the chemo treatment, her condition worsened, and she was in and out of the hospital. On one of the last days that she was in the hospital, I walked into her room and found her alone, struggling to make it to the bathroom. She was doubled over in pain and needed her hospital gown changed. I found a clean gown folded up next to her bed and helped her into it. Her frail body was limp as she held on to my arm. She could barely stand on her own. I managed to get her to the couch that was closer than the bed. I remember her lying across my lap and asking me to please just shoot her and put her out of her misery. We both cried while I stroked her thinning hair. I secretly wished I could trade bodies with her. She was eventually released from the hospital and sent home with hospice care.

Andrea returned to Phoenix to gather more things and drove back to Atlanta with her husband, Joe. I left my hotel and rented an apartment close to Michele's home for Andrea, Joe, and me. Andrea and I spent the afternoons visiting Michele. Rather than sitting up in the hospital bed that hospice had set up in her bedroom, Michele felt well enough to sit in an oversized chair at the foot of the bed facing the open windows. Her room felt light and airy with the thin white curtains flowing with the breeze. She liked looking out the two picture windows at the birds perched on the flowering dogwood tree that shaded that side of the house. Japanese spa music played from her iPad. Andrea usually sat cross-legged on the bed while I sat on the floor leaning against the wall next to Michele. Each day we claimed our spots and spent hours laughing, crying, and retelling old stories.

Michele recalled the time we made cookies and the recipe called for egg whites. She misread the recipe and told me we needed white eggs, but we only had brown eggs. We drove to the store to get a dozen white eggs and finished the batter. We realized later the misinterpretation and laughed. Michele figured we were stoned, which we probably were.

We talked about feeling grateful for having lived such full lives and how lucky we were to have made it this far, given all the crazy risks we took in our younger days. Michele reminded me of the many times we were the last ones to leave a bar after last call when the lights went on. She said she felt like it was that time. Time to move on.

We wondered what happens after this life. We talked about Thich Nhat Hanh's belief that our spiritual energy transforms when we die.[43] This energy is eternal because you can't make nothing out of something, and something out of nothing. Everything transforms, but nothing just "poof" disappears. A cloud transforms to rain, but before it was a cloud, it was vapor. She confessed that while she was a little nervous about this upcoming transformation; she thought of it as just another adventure like when we dropped acid together and jumped into another dimension. Michele said she would look for a way to communicate once she transformed, so I should be on the lookout.

---

[43] Blumberg, Antonia, "Is There Life After Death? Thich Nhat Hanh Answers Age-Old Question," Huffington Post, September 1, 2015, https://www.huffpost.com/entry/thich-nhat-hanh-life-after-death_n_55e5ff24e4b0c818f61971c7.

SHEDDING THE EARTH SUIT

As the weeks passed, Michele became weaker, and our visits became fewer. She slept most of her last days. The day before she passed, I sat by her bed while she was going in and out of consciousness. Her body was twitching at times and through her rapid breathing, she occasionally moaned. As I sat with her and held her hand, I couldn't help but think how this process of death is like birth. Her spirit was trying to find its way out and disconnect from her body like how a baby would struggle to disconnect from the mother's body. I thought about how midwives and hospice nurses were basically doing the same job. Assisting a spirit through a transition. She was at both the finish line and the starting line simultaneously.

I knew this would be my last chance to say my final goodbye, so I asked Mike if I could be alone with her. I moved in close and whispered in her ear that I was stoked she was off for another adventure and to just sit back and soak up the whole experience. I will be right behind her when my time comes. But until then, she will be in my heart every day and in the hearts of everyone she touched in this life.

I woke from my sleep early the next morning at around 2 a.m. with an abrupt alertness. I knew immediately as a prickly feeling coursed through my body that she had just passed. A few hours later, I got the call from Mike that confirmed my feelings. The harsh reality that she was forever gone set in. I wondered how I could do life without her. We did life together. Life with Michele was all I had ever known. We hung on to each other when our mother died. We shared the same crazy experiences during our teen years. She guided me out of an abusive marriage. She helped me learn how to be a mom. She was my rock when Bob passed. Looking back, I'm sure he moved me to San Diego to be close to her when he planned his final exit. She reminded me to follow my spirit while building Eddy House. She was my partner while we explored parts of the world. We walked to the veil together. She went through while I stayed behind. I tried to imagine life without her. I couldn't.

THE FIGHT INSIDE

* * *

I went back to Reno after Michele left her earth suit and knew I needed to give myself time to be present with my feelings and grieve. I packed some supplies and took off in my campervan for a couple of weeks alone in the northern California forest. Yellow butterflies seemed to be my companions throughout the entire trip. Whenever I hiked in the forest or sat at my campsite, I was accompanied by a bright yellow butterfly. Was it Michele signaling to me or was it magical thinking?

I recently went to San Diego to visit a friend. While I was there, I drove past the old apartment that once represented the dream of a new beginning. I also drove by the hospital where I said my final goodbye to Bob. It felt surreal to be in the place where Bob's spirit flamed out and mine was put to the test. I moved on from those dark days and learned the most valuable lesson of all. I learned to listen to the voice of my spirit that told me, "Nothing real can be threatened."

BONUS

OPEN-HEART MINDFULNESS TOOLBOX

This book's concepts can help you avoid a lot of unnecessary suffering and live a more intentional life. To help incorporate these ideas into your daily life, I have created the Open-Heart Mindfulness Toolbox. Here you will find tips, tools, and suggestions for bringing a greater sense of well-being and balance to your life. Download your **FREE** copy of the Toolbox here:

www.LynetteEddy.com/toolbox

ACKNOWLEDGMENTS

Many of my family members and friends contributed knowingly and unknowingly to this book. Included in this loving and supportive group are Tim Eddy, Hannah Eddy, Brian Eddy, Andrea Masnica, Jessica Hocheavar, Melanie Lewandowski, Raine Howe, Karin McCullum, Cindy Brooks, Sydney Calderon, Laurie Sunderland, Danielle Adler, Betty Scott, Kelley Smith, Donna Vaughn, Jan White, and Sharon Wilcox. This book would not have been possible without this group's support, insights, and encouragement.

Also, a warm thank you goes to Karen Karbo, who guided me through this project with patience and wisdom. A very special thank you to my dear sister, Michele. Throughout writing this book, it felt as though she was writing the words on many of these pages. While she wasn't physically sitting next to me, her spirit was close by and at the center of my heart. We wrote this book together.

ABOUT THE AUTHOR

In addition to being a MSW, Lynette Eddy is an author, social activist, and the founder of Eddy House, www.eddyhouse.org. She is a recipient of several national, state, and community awards for her achievements in social work. *The Fight Inside* is her first book. Lynette currently resides in Reno, Nevada. Visit her online at lynetteeddy.com.

www.ingramcontent.com/pod-product-compliance
Lightning Source LLC
Chambersburg PA
CBHW060527100426
42743CB00009B/1446